The Anxious Girl's Guide to Dating

How to find romance
while also being really, really nervous.

By Hattie C. Cooper

for Jared

who helped me get here

Table of Contents

Preface

When I started *The Anxious Girl's Guide to Dating* blog back in 2013, I did it for one simple reason: if I struggled with dating because of my anxiety, other people must, too. I wanted to share my experiences and connect. That, and I kept saying I wanted to start a blog about dating and anxiety and one day a friend shouted "stop f***ing whining about it and just do it." I still remember the coffee shop we were in. And the flavor of tea I tried not to cry into.

Several years later, The Anxious Girl's Guide has reached thousands of equally anxious people, most of whom find the blog by searching phrases like "nervous after first date" or "scared for first kiss" or they search "anxiety flying pooping." These are my people. I'm so thankful for all of you. Connecting with my readers and hearing your experiences has been one of my most cherished experiences. I am honored by your trust.

Now, *The Anxious Girl's Guide to Dating* comes to you in book form with highlights from the blog, even more anecdotes, a little more advice, and a lot more confessions that will have my mother asking, "Hattie, why?"

From the start I've never claimed to have all the answers. To this day I am still figuring out all the ways anxiety affects my everyday life and I am continually learning how to be a better partner. The purpose of this project is not to "fix" something. The message is not that my readers need to go on dates or need to find romance. The message is merely this: if you feel a desire to participate in the dating world and you feel your anxiety is making it difficult, you are not alone.

As always, the information I provide is from a personal perspective and should never replace the advice or care given to you by medical professionals. Please contact your doctor to discuss how best to cope with anxiety and depression. Each individual has a unique set of needs.

And please, if you are experiencing suicidal thoughts, contact the suicide hotline at
1-800-273-8255. They are open 24/7. Know this: never feel alone.

Thank you for spending some time with me and thank you for your continued support of *The Anxious Girl's Guide to Dating*. I appreciate you more than you know.
xo,
Hattie

Introduction

My Anxiety & My Heart:

They Just Can't Leave Each Other Alone

"Can you describe what it felt like?"

The doctor stood at the foot of my hospital bed, pushing at my ankles and feeling my shins. An assistant placed sticky plastic circles around my chest.

I tried not to fidget. "Like my left boob was suddenly detaching from my body."

Cracking a smile, I waited for the laugh that never came. The doctor just continued pushing at my legs. But, I mean, come on. The mental image of a breast falling from a body, like a college student marching out of a dull philosophy class, flipping the bird and shouting "I don't need this." It'd felt like my breast didn't want to listen to my musings on life anymore.

Earlier that day I'd called my general doctor's office. I'd been experiencing odd tightness in my chest. Mild nausea. Fatigue. These were all symptoms I'd experienced off and on since childhood — symptoms that are familiar to anyone living with anxiety. Another doctor told me in

1

college I probably have Generalized Anxiety Disorder, but really, I'm just always nervous. So when I called my doctor, it was in hopes of getting a general checkup. I wasn't feeling great.

But the real reason was the boob thing. A few days before, I'd been in the shower and suddenly felt like my left breast had detached from my skin. Like a fork was jammed against my ribs. I'd even looked down, expecting to see a crooked set of breasts. Instead, I was met with the same sight as always. An average set of breasts and my pale skin being coaxed to a shade of red usually reserved for flowers in Shakespearean sonnets.

The doctor's office told me I needed to visit an ER. They told me I could have blood clots.

My brain said, "pssh, it's just my anxiety, I'm fine," but my anxiety said "yep, it's finally happened. The cancer found you. Start Googling how to draft a will."

As I sat in the hospital bed, the technician performing an EKG, the assistant botching the IV, *whoops let me try the other arm*, I kept explaining how I had anxiety. I pointed out all the tests felt excessive. I sat there and tried not to roll my eyes at myself. At my patterns. At the fact that my entire life has been dominated by my anxiety, my desire to be cautious, and my poor, desperate, heart.

My anxiety and my heart have been intertwined since childhood.

From elementary school and into adulthood I can see how my anxiety has directly affected my romantic life.

Negative thought patterns, excessive worry, over-analyzing everything, avoidant behavior, depression, isolation, fear, the majority of my actions coming from a buried seed of fear that bloomed into a friggin' redwood tree of control over my life. Do you know what I mean?

And now, here I was once more. Being wheeled across the hall in a thin fabric hospital gown, being asked to stand in front of a white metal box while the doctor X-Rayed everything held warm and safe within my ribcage. Here I was, once again, over-analyzing everything going on in my heart.

I wasn't surprised. The previous month I'd quit my decent-paying job at a tech startup in Seattle to pursue my writing, a move that both baffled and concerned the same people who had applauded me almost exactly a year prior when I landed the job. "What a lucky break for someone with a Master's in poetry," they'd said, as if thankful they could all sleep better knowing I wasn't moving to Paris to try and sell poetry outside the Moulin Rouge. Breathe easy, folks. The poet has been contained.

The same month I quit my job, my boyfriend Jared proposed to me. Something that, for a pessimist like myself, was more anxiety-producing than squeal-inducing. I knew I wanted to share my life with this man, but the idea of an elaborate engagement and wedding made me want to furiously dig a hole in the background, crawl in, and pull a camouflage sheet over the top. *Don't look at me*, my hand-painted sign would say.

I was unemployed, expected to plan a wedding, and was flying to Virginia the following week to attend the wedding of my sister. A lot was going on. So, naturally, this would be reflected in how blood circulated in my body.

After the test results came back, I waited to hear the doctor scream cancer at me like a carnival barker. But instead, he was calm.

"We've ruled out all the major concerns," the doctor told me. He held a small stack of papers and read from them.

"Your symptoms are most likely anxiety related. Take one of your Ativan's when you feel like you need it."

I was left alone, the paperwork explaining what anxiety was, telling me to contact my primary care physician, and suggesting I take a pill. I took a few shaky breaths and told myself it was a good thing. I was lucky to be walking into known territory. I am familiar with my anxiety. It has been my constant companion since childhood.

The poet Jericho Brown once said he believes "every poem is a love poem." And I feel this is also true for every person who lives with anxiety. Your story, is a love story. Your experiences help you learn how to love yourself and the world around you. The pain, setbacks, and frustrations you may experience from your anxiety are all helping you better understand yourself. This, in turn, will teach you truths. And this, in the end, will lead you to truer love. I believe this. And it is why I started *The Anxious Girl's Guide to Dating* in the first place.

Chapter 1

Seeking Connection and Understanding

It Is Okay To Want a Connection

My grandfather passed away when I was in elementary school. Years later, when I was in college and visiting my grandmother, I remember sitting with her and discussing a man I had a crush on. Having never remarried, she spent a great deal of time in solitude and as she listened to me describe the man I liked, she nodded and said, "It's just nice to have someone to talk to about your day, isn't it? That's what I miss the most. Just talking about my day with someone."

And through the mess of all my crushes, my failed dates, and bruised emotions, I remember this. That, above all, I would like someone with whom I can simply talk about my day. Someone who will listen. Someone who will share their day with me.

When I first started writing for *The Anxious Girl's Guide to Dating* blog, I worried that by simply giving dating advice I was sending a message to readers that they should be dating. I was a late bloomer and know firsthand how abrasive it can feel for someone to act as if they know more about my heart than I do.

Above everything else, I believe my readers should follow their gut and live their life in the truest, most honest way possible. Whatever this looks like for you as an individual, I encourage you to follow what feels most closely aligned with how you want your life to look.

However, I also know my grandma was onto something. It is human to crave connection, to be drawn to community, intimacy, and being known by other people. We develop friendships as early as infancy and continue to develop friendships throughout our lives. It is okay to want to be in a romantic relationship. Is it weird that I'm even saying this?

I remember feeling stubborn as a late bloomer. I bristled at anyone telling me I should start dating. I rolled my eyes at people who talked incessantly about wanting to get married. There was a small part of me that took pride in not "needing" to be in a relationship. But there was an even smaller, softer, yet somehow louder part of me that often marched up to me in the middle of the night and shouted that I wanted to share my life with someone.

I wanted to talk with someone about my day.

There is no weakness in wanting to be known by another person. Wanting to share your days with someone else is different than needing to. It took me years to understand this difference. And it's quite possible that my anxiety, and all the fears that come along with it, were behind the stubbornness I felt in being single.

While it may not be the case for you, try and understand if you associate wanting to be in a relationship with any negative associations. Being aware of how we perceive relationships can inform how we approach the pursuit of one.

Defining Your Anxiety

It has taken me years of living with anxiety to even begin to try and understand how I define it. I believe the best way to take back control of your life is through education. Learn as much as you possibly can about yourself. Give it a name. Understand how it affects your thoughts and behaviors and make small adjustments accordingly.

For me, one way I've come to look at my anxiety is I imagine I'm like a balloon. The air inside me is my anxiety. It is what helps give me shape. When I start to gain control over one aspect of the anxiety, compress it, squeeze the spot until I think I've forced it gone, the anxiety finds its way into another area of my life. The air just shifts. It still pops out. I can manipulate the form the anxiety comes in, but it will always be there. Knowing the inevitably of my anxiety being present in my everyday life prepares me for the vigilance I need in learning about it.

When I first was given a full name for what I was experiencing, I was in my junior year of college. My every day anxiety was escalating out of my control as I tried to start dating a handsome, intelligent, biology major, who also happened to Irish step dance. I was smitten. And I also recently told him that I was too nervous to eat in front of him. The conversation went something like this:

Him: Why aren't you eating your dinner – does it taste weird?
Me: (looks down at untouched meal he bought me) No, it's fine.
Him: Do you want something else?
Me: I'm afraid if I eat I will throw up on you.
Him: Do you want to make out and frolic on the beach?*

*some statements have been edited to create more sexy tension in the scene.

I cried a lot during those few weeks of trying to date that man. Frustrated by my reaction to a simple meal with a very nice, very agile, Irish jigger, I went to the campus clinic. After filling out a few questionnaires (on a scale from rarely to as frequent as the sun rising, how often do you get diarrhea?) a nondescript doctor told me I suffer from Generalized Anxiety Disorder.

To me, I imagine my Generalized Anxiety Disorder as a creature external of myself. Like a large, hairy, bright red creature not unlike Sasquatch. He sleeps in the corner of my bedroom. I can hear the light whistle of his breath as I lay in the dark. Sometimes he wakes up and stands over me. Sometimes he follows me out of the apartment as I go about my day. Sometimes he barges into parties, meetings at work, or plops down in the seat next to me on an airplane. I try to tell myself he is harmless. One day I will tie his shoe laces together and watch him stumble as he tries to chase me.

The actual clinical definition can be found below:

Generalized Anxiety Disorder
From the DSM - IV, the diagnostic manual used by medical professionals

A. Excessive anxiety and worry (apprehensive expectation), occurring more days than not and for at least 6 months, about a number of events or activities.

B. The person finds it difficult to control the worry

C. The anxiety and worry are associated with three (or more) of the following six symptoms:

(1) restlessness or feeling keyed up or on edge

(2) being easily fatigued

(3) difficulty concentrating or mind going blank

(4) irritability

(5) muscle tension

(6) sleep disturbance

D. The focus of the anxiety and worry is not confined to features of an Axis I disorder

E. The anxiety, worry, or physical symptoms cause clinically significant distress or impairment in social, occupational, or other important areas of functioning.

F. The disturbance is not due to the direct physiological effects of a substance or general medical condition and does not occur exclusively during a mood disorder, a psychotic disorder or a pervasive developmental disorder.

While DSM definitions are always helpful as starting points, you will get to know your own anxiety more intimately over the years. Unlike the DSM definition, you will start unearthing all the complexities and intricate layers that come along with your own form of anxiety. You may find that your anxiety is like an unwelcome houseguest, barging in the front door, throwing its body on the couch and laughing in your face when you politely ask it to leave.

Or maybe you'll learn to greet your anxiety with open arms, welcome it as if it is an old friend. Maybe, instead of fearing your anxiety or resenting it, you simply smile. "Haven't seen you in a few days," you might hear yourself saying. And then, satisfied to know it hasn't been forgotten, your anxiety evaporates again.

No matter how you learn to recognize and define your anxiety, it's important that you do. By learning more about yourself you continue to grow. In this growth you will fine-tune your ability to share yourself with another person. In the end, the better you understand your anxiety the better you will be able to talk to someone, connect with someone, at the end of the day.

Chapter 2

Late Blooming

Like a Kickass Butterfly Who Wants to Make a Sexy Grand Entrance

Never underestimate the importance and value of knowing yourself. Of truly knowing who you are as an individual. Spend a few moments trying to think how you would define yourself. If I were to ask you to describe yourself, what words would you use? Does the fact that you're a late-bloomer affect how you see yourself?

Anyone who has attempted to fill out an online dating profile knows the dreaded "tell us about yourself!" section that forces you to try and explain your complex personality in a few words. It's always awkward talking about yourself (I am a cool person, trust me. No seriously, you can trust me because I'm cool). As uncomfortable as the experience might be, it's always important to try and understand how you see yourself.

For example, there are people who only know themselves as one half of a romantic relationship (Married to the best hubby in the world!!!!!!).

There are people who only know themselves as defined by their career (Associate Executive to the Supreme Leader of Everything).

Some people would be lost without being defined as an athlete, a musician, a high-power executive, or a straight-A student.

If you're a late bloomer, you might feel it is part of your identity. I know I felt it was a significant part of who I was. If so, then you're part of a fortunate group. One of the only ways to truly know yourself, as an individual, is through solitude. There is a difference between loneliness and solitude, which we'll explore soon. But the sooner we remind ourselves how vital it is to have alone time the sooner we can let go of the notion that everyone "should" be in a relationship.

Why Being a Late Bloomer is the Best

Throughout my teenage years, and even now as an adult, I felt like a late bloomer. I remember looking around and wondering, "Why is every single person I know in a relationship? Even that guy who wears t-shirts covered in penis cartoons has a girlfriend." Then I'd go back to brushing my cat and reading Sylvia Plath.

Just the other day I was sitting with Jared, trying to explain to him how I feel a lot younger. How we feel a lot younger, as a couple. Despite nearing our thirties and planning a very adult future together (we're hoping to maybe have kids when?) we still feel young. It's the first serious relationship for both of us. This means we have a lot left to learn about our individual relationship styles. There's a lot left to learn about each other.

12

I didn't have my first kiss until I was 22. At the time it felt like I was the last human on earth to not be kissed. Hell, I was the last creature with a mouth who hadn't been kissed — I saw how often those Real Housewives kiss their Pomeranians on the lips; I mean, seriously?

I love being a late bloomer.

This may sound like a defense mechanism. Like I'm someone who took a wrong turn and as we drive along a backroad reserved for hill people and serial killers, I sweep my arms and declare, "Look at this beautiful scenery we wouldn't have seen otherwise!" But I mean it. I wouldn't trade being a late bloomer for anything.

While friends of mine jumped from one relationship to the next, developing a fear of being single, I have the deep knowledge that I am fine on my own. I was able to truly get to know myself over my years of solitude. Through this I'm better able communicate my needs, fears, and hopes to future partners.

This doesn't mean being single for so long didn't come with its challenges. I often felt insecure and unloved. I often questioned why nobody had ever made a strong effort to be with me. I often felt like one of those roly-poly bugs, curled into myself, with fear and a desire for comfort.

Family get-togethers were a creature of judgement all on their own. They were a special time for home-cooked meals, gift-giving, and routine questions about my love life.

"Is there anyone special in your life right now?" A well-meaning relative would ask, eyes sparkling with a combination of hope and panic.

I remember preparing my canned answers on the drives over. And while I honestly can't remember specifics, it's probably safe to say I lied every once in a while just to have something new to say. "He's studying to be a doctor," I probably said with a manic grin.

We will cover family and friends more in Chapter Eight, but as you bloom later, try your best to quiet the judgmental voices. The voices that whisper you're doing it wrong.

This voice may come from your family or friends. But sometimes this voice comes from your own mind. You might become your own worst cheerleader, messing up the routine, falling from the sky, and forgetting to wear your underwear. Stop. Just stop. Train yourself to be the most kickass cheerleader for yourself possible. You may not have control over the things said by other people but you can control how and why you support yourself.

Remind yourself that you are practicing solitude, which is something our contemporary society of attached-to-our-smartphones desperately needs more often. You have the opportunity to become the best possible version of yourself before you decide to take new steps into the dating world. Raise this flag high and watch it flapping with color and life in the wind.

Taking New Steps & Rewarding Yourself

One of the ways I've learned to gently encourage myself to take new steps is through rewards. It is like I am training myself. Plain and simple.

Do something scary? Get a treat. Try something new? Get a treat. Do this over and over and over again until those scary steps became comfortable. Let's take a moment and remember Pavlov's Dog. In the late 1800s a physiologist, Ivan Pavlov, stumbled across the building blocks of classical conditioning. Pavlov rang a bell every time he fed his dog. And soon, just the sound of the bell made the dog salivate. He became conditioned.

We can do this to ourselves. We can train ourselves to salivate at the thought of taking new steps.

Mmm, tasty new steps.

I don't make a big production out of my reward system, but I always pause to be proud of myself for doing something new or scary. Regardless of whether or not the outside world identifies it as "scary," I listen to my gut and allow myself to feel my feelings. Then I buy myself some motherfuckin' flowers like I'm James effing Bond.

When I started dating one of my first real-life boyfriends I was a nervous wreck. I was 25, inexperienced, and sweaty as hell all the time. Even the act of walking to his apartment would cause me anxiety. So, as a reward, I would buy myself a small bouquet of carnations on my walk back home. Carnations were cheap so I didn't feel guilty about spending money. And they are the cockroaches of flowers: they live forever. Win, win.

As the flowers bloomed they were physical reminders of my own growth. I could look at their soft color and remember I'd been bold.

Your reward doesn't have to be flowers. Maybe taking a hike or bringing a good friend to coffee feels like a treat. No matter what, identify something small, affordable, and simple that brings you joy. Use that. Over time this will help encourage you to be bolder and bolder and soon, just like my carnations, you'll be blossoming more than you thought possible and maybe even become invincible because seriously? Those damn flowers never die.

Setting Your Goals

Maybe you know you want to start taking new steps, but you aren't sure of your exact destination yet. Maybe you know you want a relationship, but haven't figured out what that means for you. Maybe you're overwhelmed by the thought of trying to define what you want. Do all these questions make you want to stop trying before you even begin?

Take a deep breath. Step back. Stop expecting so much of yourself. Big change occurs with very small, very achievable, steps. Sometimes changing just one habit from your day can transform your life. Before anything, make sure your desire for change comes from your heart and not from outside pressure or expectations. Just because your great aunt Wanda keeps telling you that you need to find a nice girl and settle down, doesn't mean that's what you need to do. However, if you do truly crave a new direction, remind yourself you have a choice in the matter. You hold the key to opening that door.

Here's where I usually start: with an image.

It's as easy as that.

Ignoring what I think my goal "should" be in life, I instead start searching around for an image that speaks to my gut. Something that pulls at me for one reason or another. Your intuition knows more than you might realize.

Let's go back in time a few years: It was New Year's 2013. I was single and knew I wanted to start dating. As I sat with a pad of paper in hand, the words New Year's Resolutions staring me in the face, I hated the idea of writing down something about dating. It felt so cliché to be 26, single, and writing "this year I will find a nice boyfriend."

But then I thought of something a friend once said. I'd overheard her talking about her partner in a way that stuck with me. She told me he "made her soul feel good." While the phrasing maybe sounded cheesier than a fondue restaurant, it rang true to me. I wanted to be with someone who made my soul feel good. Which, when you think about it, is a pretty tall order. What does that even mean exactly? How do you quantify that?

So instead of listing my goal as boyfriend-dating-oriented, I made my New Year's Resolution to be to "find someone who makes my soul feel good."

To help myself focus on this abstract idea, I went looking for an image to reflect it. I found a few pictures that made me feel filled with joy, ease, and light. I made one of these images the background of my computer and taped the other on my refrigerator, two places I knew I'd see them every day. By placing these images in my line of sight it was as if I was setting my intention every day. Today I intend to seek joy, to seek ease, and to seek light.

Soon, these images became background noise. I forgot their purpose. And as the weeks rolled by I started to feel depressed that I wasn't more engaged with the dating world.

But then, at the end of January, I met a man who I felt at ease around. He seemed to emit joy, a quick smile flashing across his face with as much authenticity as a newborn baby. As the night came to a close, I said goodbye to him feeling lighter. I remember us both walking to our separate cars, the street and sidewalk dusted with snow, and I remember feeling like I wanted to be around him more. I didn't want to say goodbye to the goodness he made me feel. This man is still my partner and he wants to share his life with me. And to this day I still feel lighter when I'm around him.

If you're not sure where to start, start with your gut. How do you want to feel? What images in the world reflect this? Spend some time soaking in these images every day. The more you absorb the importance of those emotions, the more likely you are to notice them when they come along in real life.

From Our Readers
I've decided I want to change some things in my life . . . mainly, I want this to be the year I finally get out of my shell and actually go on a few dates, but I'm worried I won't follow through. What would you suggest I do?

A friend told me about a sign she saw at her local Burger stand: "May your troubles last as long as your New Year's Resolutions."

For some reason, we have a hard time sticking to our goals. Everyone does. Changing our habits often seems simple, yet turns out to be daunting. We are creatures of routine and it takes a lot of persistence and accountability to switch up that routine.

We often tell ourselves:

This year I'm going to visit the gym every day before work (*snooze button*snooze button*)

This is the year I'm going to start eating less meat (Gimme those fried chicken wings)

By the end of the year I'll have written the first draft of that novel I keep wanting to write (celebrity gossip websites here I come!)

So for starters, don't beat yourself up. We all want to grow and have the best intentions, but then life gets in the way. Here's what I'd suggest: break down your goals. Change just one, simple, habit from your daily life.

We tend to make big sweeping declarations when we want to change something in our life. We make big statements like "this year I'll have my first kiss!" or "this year I'm going on at least one date each month!"

What's tricky about these statements is they can feel daunting, overwhelming, or absolutely exhausting. It can result in simply putting it off. The fear of failure is often more powerful than our desire for change. Be aware of this.

Break each resolution down into manageable steps. Then remember to feel proud of yourself for achieving each step. Maybe one step will be to simply research different online dating sites. The next could be opening up a profile. The next is filling out that awkward profile. Maybe turn the task into a fun activity with a friend.

When you break down your goal into smaller, more manageable steps you can look back over the weeks and see all these small steps you've taken versus beating yourself up for not achieve the "one big goal." I know that I wouldn't be dating the kind man that I am if it weren't for hundreds of baby steps and learning, evaluating, growing, growing, growing, all the growing I've done in my past. Break down your goals into smaller, more attainable, goals. And remember that true change is often so gradual we don't even notice it's occurred.

Loneliness vs. Solitude

There is a difference between loneliness and solitude.
Often, the people around you may assume you are lonely if you are single. I remember a friend once asking, "Don't you get lonely?"
The truth was, yes. I got lonely. But here's another truth: I still get lonely. Even while being part of a relationship.
Loneliness is an inherent and basic human emotion. We experience the feeling regardless of whether or not we are in a relationship. Loneliness comes from missing something or someone, whether it's the friendships you had in high school, your parents who have since passed, or your

19

childhood home. It's inaccurate to think that being in a relationship will suddenly cure you of ever feeling lonely again. The minute we start thinking another person can rid us of loneliness forever is the minute we lose sight of what it means to be human.

I've known people who from the outside appear to be in a healthy relationship, but on the inside they feel unable to speak freely. The feel like they have to hide their true personalities, which results in them not feeling known. They are lonely despite being in a relationship.

My many years of being the perpetual single person in my friend group allowed me years of valuable solitude. And this is dramatically different than loneliness.

Loneliness comes from a place of feeling incomplete and being disconnected. Solitude is a place for connection.

Solitude allows you to process what you are experiencing in life. It gives you the space and time to better understand how you feel. It allows you to evaluate, weigh, and adjust your values.

I went to college near the ocean and would often get in my car and drive out to one of the smaller, less touristy beaches. I'd usually wear long sleeves, long pants, and close-toed shoes since I burned so easily. I walked amongst the bikini-clad girls like a nun praying for all the heathens around her (just kidding. I was totally jealous of their tans).

This particular place had a swing set on the beach. As I pumped my feet, sand kicking up from the bottom of my shoes, I felt like I was flying above the waves. I tended to visit these swings when I felt weighed down by my thoughts or anxiety. I'd feel the sharp salt air in my face, the warmth of the sun, and feel sorry for myself like it was my job and someone was paying me a lot of money to feel sorrier and sorrier. But more than that, I was giving myself time to be with myself and to try and understand why I was feeling a certain way. Usually, I was hurting from an epic crush who didn't know I existed.

Even if these moments of solitude may have been a form of dwelling or a very sunscreened pity-party, they were special. I was allowing myself to be present. A lot of people are uncomfortable with stillness and being alone with their thoughts. A lot of people seek distractions like television or video games or take part in avoidant behaviors such as drinking or partying.

It takes strength to be present in solitude. And it will build a strong foundation for your personality as you draw closer to being ready to try the dating world. Never feel weak or embarrassed for being alone. You have the gift of being able to truly know yourself. This is a gift you can share with someone else when the time is right.

How to Embrace Being a Late Bloomer

1
Solitude is an important and healthy way for you to center yourself and truly understand how you relate to the world around you.

2
Remember: Being part of a relationship does not automatically cure loneliness.

3
Your values, beliefs, and personality should be shaped by you alone.

4
You always have the choice to start seeking change, when you are ready.

5

Reward yourself when you achieve something new.
Acknowledge your growth.

Chapter 3

Let's Talk About Talking:

How to Talk Good and Other Flirty Word Things

I signed up for Speech 101 my first semester of community college. It was a pre-requisite and I figured it would be an easy class to get out of the way. On the first day of the semester I sat in the back listening to my classmates chatter nervously. Everyone quickly made the connection that they'd waited until their last possible semester to take the class. Everyone spent years dreading it.

"I almost contemplated not graduating just to avoid Speech," joked a guy wearing his wallet on a chain. Everyone nodded or laughed, understanding his thought process.

As I soon learned in my Speech class, public speaking is the top-rated fear among Americans. It ranks higher than death. Death.

Speaking in public makes you feel exposed. It makes you feel vulnerable. Even people without everyday anxiety can experience the symptoms of anxiety because of public speaking. Accelerated heartrate, sweaty palms, nausea, dizziness, and dry mouth are all symptoms people may feel.

Despite my generalized anxiety, public speaking doesn't really bother me. Maybe because I spend 99% of the rest of my day freaking the shit out about every small thing so giving a speech in front of some randos doesn't feel that bad. At least I am in control. At least I know what to expect.

But while I never cared much about speaking in public, you may as well have notified FEMA when it came to my ability to talk to boys I liked. I was always a disaster.

I blushed. I shook. I panicked. I wanted to hide. I sometimes did hide. When I did, it was usually in bathrooms.

I would overcompensate for my in-person nerves with obscure and out-of-the-blue messages on social media. I once emailed a guy and asked him what kind of leaf he would be if he could be any kind of leaf. I wish I could say my bedroom talk has improved since this message time in my life, but Jared recently had to answer the question "did you hear me fart just now?"

I once chugged a beer before going to a literature class where I had a crush on an enigmatic writer. I left class early since I felt sick and self-conscious. I spent the entire bus ride home crying.

This is all to say, talking to someone you find attractive is difficult. It pushes you outside of your comfort zone. It can sometimes make you miserable. But I know this to be true: the more you take baby steps the more those muscles will develop. If you want to push yourself, you will someday be able to run a marathon. I am telling you this from my heart — you are capable of doing this.

Surviving the Three Minutes of Terror & Small Talk

When our body feels under threat it triggers the fight or flight reaction. When encountering a situation that is scary to us (like dating or talking to someone cute) our bodies automatically jump into survival mode. Sweating, difficulty breathing, nausea, jumbled thoughts . . . basically our bodies betray us when we most need to be "cool."

But here's the thing: after about three minutes our bodies realize we are not in immediate danger and will automatically start to calm down. This survival mode was developed as a means, through evolution, to be aware of actual external threats. Big animals, inclement weather, and literal enemies who might try to steal everything we just hunted and gathered throughout the day – in my imagination these are all the threats for which our fight or flight mode was developed.

But now, that same physiological reaction often crops up in unnecessary moments. Typically the most stressful and difficult part of talking to someone is that moment when you first walk up. It's the buildup of the unknowns you feel yourself moving towards them. The fear comes from all the uncertainty. The fight or flight is triggered when you first open your mouth and when you're scrambling to think of anything to say. And for a few minutes, it's just pure agony.

Oftentimes the fear of this moment prevents us from even trying. But if you push yourself to take those first few steps you'll find yourself in the moment. You'll be smack in the middle of it. And soon, you'll realize that even if it sucks, you're not dead. You'll get through it. Then, lucky you, you get to do the dance of small talk which, if you're anything like me, is the sweatiest dance you have to dance in your life.

One of the main reasons I dislike professional networking events (or, you know, any kind of event) is my dislike of small talk. Small talk makes me squirm. It feels empty and uncomfortable. My tongue suddenly feels too big for my mouth and it loses basic motor function. I slur my speech.

For someone with anxiety, small talk tends to increase symptoms of anxiety. Unfortunately when you first start dating someone you usually have to endure small talk. This may make you want to avoid the dating scene all together.

When I tried to enter the dating world I remember wanting to make a t-shirt that said "I'm a writer. I grew up in California. I have one sister and, yes, the weather was nice today." People always want to know what you do for a living. Where you grew up. What your family is like. And if you happened to notice the weather that day.

But you know what? I find myself asking these exact damn questions of people when I meet them. There's no escaping it.

If you suffer from small-talk anxiety when it comes to dating, try and remember this: often the person asking you these questions feels mild anxiety as well. Small talk is a form of comfort-seeking, both on the part of the question'er and the question'ee. The person asking the questions may have no idea what else to say. Or they don't know you well enough to ask more probing questions and want to make sure you feel comfortable. Tell yourself you are doing the person a favor by answering their small-talk questions. Just as they may be easing you into a conversation, you are also helping them in return.

If you find yourself frustrated by the lack of depth in these conversations, spend some time developing more interesting questions. Think of follow-up questions you can ask after the expected ones. For example, if they tell you they have two younger brothers you could ask if they all got along as children. Or if they tell you they work in sales, ask if that was what they thought they'd be doing at this point in life.

Either way, remember that every close friendship you have most likely started off with a little small talk.

Flirting & Asking Someone Out

I can't tell you how many times I've heard people say statements like, "Oh man, I'm so awkward when I try to flirt." I know, because I was guilty of saying it.

I've heard this sentence come from people who, from the outside, appear completely cool and relaxed. I've heard it from people who are witty and charming. I've heard it from people who – from my perspective – could be runway models.

Flirting can be uncomfortable for even the smoothest of people. Sure, there will always be people who are cocky and gregarious, but I can bet you a whole pile of non-Monopoly money they still have a small voice in their head that whispers insecurities.

Awkwardness can be charming in its own way. It can help release tension since the other person may not feel as much pressure to also appear chill. My advice for flirting is to always be genuine and just a little self-deprecating. Don't be afraid to put yourself out there in hopes of helping the other person feel more at ease.

Trying to be someone you're not will only increase your anxiety. It will create the pressure to be "on" and it will instill a fear of relaxing into your more natural personality. You may even become ashamed of your true personality.

So much of the anxiety about flirting comes from the core belief that we are not worthy of attention or love. If we spend years loathing our anxiety and fearing it makes us unlovable, it may be hard to then share ourselves with another person.

Don't quote me on this, but hypothetically I might say something cliché here like "you have to love yourself before you can love someone else." Or something like that.

But it's true. This is why people say it and why it has become a cliché. Because as years go on and history repeats itself and people try to connect, we continually come around to the same ah-ha moment, like we're discovering it for the first time. How will anyone else like me if I don't even like myself?

Flirting should come from a place of sincerity. Your sincerity comes from a place of feeling secure and confident in yourself as an individual. Own your quirks and embrace what makes you unique. The more you learn to live a fulfilling life as a single person, becoming the best version of yourself possible, the more you will be able to share yourself with another person.

If you are talking to someone you like, be genuine. Ask questions. Listen. Have fun. Ask more questions. If they aren't reciprocating with an equal degree of authenticity don't allow it to be a setback. Do the best you can and don't stop.

If you find yourself liking someone enough to ask them out on a date, remember the same concepts from when we discussed first talking with someone. Asking someone out will probably trigger your fight or flight response.

Asking someone out is scary for anyone. But if you are cripplingly shy or nervous or anxious it can feel downright impossible. Plus, there's the added layer that if the person says "yes" you'll then have to actually hang out with them and talk to them and pretend to be normal and talk about your likes and dislikes and *pulls hood over face*.

It's such a funny dichotomy when you start looking at our deep, organic, heart-based desire to connect compared to our primal, pure and honest reaction of pure terror at the idea of actually having to hang out with someone. THANKS BRAIN CHEMICALS.

So here's my advice for someone who is trying to figure out how in the bloody hell to ask someone out on a date:

Step 1
Get to know the person a little bit first

If they sit near you in Humanities 101 ask them about an assignment. Comment on something they have (a bag, shirt, phone, etc) to spark conversation. Ask them about other classes. Compliment them. Be deeply true to yourself which will help the person see the real you. Being yourself will also remind you that you're capable of talking to the person without dying. If you're thinking *hey, Hattie, thanks a lot for the awesome tip, but I can't even get up the nerve to talk to this person in the first place! Then you really need to start here. Start by talking to them.* About anything. It's as easy and horrifying as that. Just go do it. Take a deep breath and step off the high-dive. Removing "asking someone out" from the equation entirely and replacing it with "just getting to know them as a person" reprioritizes the pressure.

Step 2
Find a natural "next step"

Has the person mentioned how much they love jazz? Or how much they've been dying to try that new Tiki Bar downtown? Or do they constantly post photos online of succulents? No matter what, keep your ears open for items that lead to natural next steps. This keeps the stakes low and creates a smoother transition into the next step.

Step 3
Use social media and technology

Let's be real for a sec' . . . social media and technology dominates the dating world right now. And don't even get me started on how much texting has changed the face of dating. I know a lot of people hold tight to more classic, old-school ways of dating, but really? As an anxious person I would be much more comfortable with someone asking me out with a text message than him showing up in a suit with a bouquet of flowers and a singing teddy bear. With a text I have time to process and don't have to worry about using the correct facial expression.

Step 4
Give yourself permission to leave it undefined at the beginning

I remember, all too clearly, a few "hang outs" I had where afterwards I sat there wondering "wait....was that a date?" And then my friends would ask me about it and I felt stupid for not knowing and it'd be awkward. But here's the thing: if you enjoy a person's company and they enjoy your company you will naturally end up spending more and more time together getting to know each other. While, yes, you should probably (eventually) have an honest conversation about what each person hopes for the relationship, at first allow it to be what it is.

Here's the obvious thing that sucks about wanting to spend more time with someone: they may not reciprocate the feeling. This can really, oh man really, hurt. And there's only so much you can do about that. But that doesn't mean you shouldn't push yourself to do something scary, be bold and go for something you want in life. When we face a scary situation we learn about our own strength and character. We grow and we prepare for future scenarios when the timing will be right.

If you aren't ready to try quite yet, then ask yourself when. When will the situation ever be "perfect?" Go do something you maybe think you can't and then buy yourself a damn cookie or something.

Voicing Fears & Feeling Safe

I'm afraid of the woods at night.
I'm afraid of being stuck on a plane, on the tarmac, for hours on end.
I'm afraid of getting diarrhea in a place where there's no restroom.
I'm afraid of falling in the shower.
I was a fearful child and I am still a fearful adult.
I've always found ease in vocalizing my fears and insecurities or I did until I ended up in a long-term committed relationship.
For some reason I am afraid (see? even more fear) to say some things out loud. Particularly I'm afraid of voicing my fears for our relationship. To physically release the thoughts, to sit and listen to them coming out of my mouth, felt dangerous. As if the words themselves would cling to the walls of our home, spawn, multiply, and infect the very air we breathe every day.
I am a firm believer in identifying areas of your life you want to improve, making a plan for how to approach the changes, then moving forward boldly. I believe change and positive growth is possible. We, as humans, have been given the gift of free will and dammit we better take advantage of that! Except, sometimes we can't.

31

Maybe this makes me a control freak, but the things I can't control in life scare me the most. As in, I can't predict or control whether or not a tumor chooses to form in the body of a person I love. I can't control the weather when we drive. I can't control your heart.

I also know I can't control another person, which becomes most illuminated when you're dating someone.

I fear infidelity. Both on the part of my partner and in myself. The heart is such a mysterious and complex organ that I sometimes find myself worrying about scenarios down the road where it's being tested.

For the longest time I couldn't bring myself to talk about this with Jared. There was a part of me that felt even holding this fear spoke to something deeper and uglier. There was a part of me that didn't want him thinking I didn't trust him. And there was a part of me that felt it conveyed a lack of faith, on my part, in the strength of our relationship.

So I carried the fear silently for a long time. Until, one night, I just started talking about it. And it ended up not being a big deal because, news flash, it's not like Jared didn't know infidelity exists in the world. We both know multiple couples who have dealt with it in various forms. It's a reality of intimate relationships.

Speaking the fear out loud shrunk the size and weight of it; it gave me, and my significant other, the power back.

Vulnerability can be the scariest thing of all. If information is power, then letting someone in on some of our most intimate pieces of information gives them a lot of power. It's like we're sliding a manila envelope, containing all our deepest secrets, across a table. They now hold that envelope in their hands and we can only pray they don't lose it.

Anyone who ever made a pinky-promise with a friend in elementary school, the other person whispering, *I'll never to tell a soul*, knows that trusting someone can easily go to shit. Those pinky-promises only worked like 45% of the time. People can use your trust against you, manipulate you, or hurt you. There's no sugar coating it, people can suck.

But if you are pursuing a relationship with someone who genuinely wants the two of you to succeed, voicing your fears will only strengthen the connection. It shows faith in the other person, and in the relationship, to acknowledge that it won't always be perfect. Take some time trying to understand what you're afraid to say. Try to understand why you're afraid to talk about the subject. Then, just start talking.

Saying Thank You When You Want to Say Sorry

My anxiety, and the ways it directly affects my social skills, results in a fair amount of self-loathing. I find myself disliking parts of myself that I imagine outside people view as "annoying."

I find myself worrying that the aspects of my personality I find most difficult are also the aspects others find difficult. It was not hard for me to convince myself (especially towards the beginning of our relationship) that Jared would rather be with someone who is "easier" to live with.

It's at these times I find myself wanting to apologize for my behavior. I'm sorry I am so difficult. I'm sorry I cry so easily. I'm sorry I don't always want to go meet up for drinks with friends, I'm sorry that I am, I'm sorry, I'm sorry I —

Except don't.

First off, you should not have to apologize for who you are. While, yes, sometimes our behavior results in situations where an apology is needed and justified, continual apologies for your personality will only reinforce your own insecurities.

Second, it forces your partner into a tough situation. When you apologize they may feel obligated to tell you it's okay, or not to worry about it, or that they are sorry too. None of this may be necessary, or even healthy, for your communication.

Instead? Say thank you.

Thank you for being so patient with me. Thank you for giving me the safe space to cry. Thank you for respecting my need for alone time.

This reminds your partner that they are appreciated. It reminds them their actions are noticed. And it reminds the other person their behavior towards you makes you feel loved and understood. which will reinforce more of that behavior.

I've been trying to catch myself more and more when the word sorry is on the tip of my tongue. I try to evaluate where the apology is coming from. Taking just five seconds to understand if the apology is coming from a place of insecurity can help redirect a moment towards healthier outcomes. I try to remember to thank Jared for loving me when I'm emotional, anxious, or conflicted.

Pay attention to your apology habits in the next few weeks. Try and see if you have a knee-jerk reaction to apologize any time you do anything you fear may be received unfavorably. Then stop yourself and say thank you instead. The more you practice saying thank you the faster you will learn you don't need to apologize for who you are.

And to you, my readers, thank you for reading.

How to Be Open & Honest

1

Always be honest with yourself first, even if it is scary.

2
Remember that honesty begets honesty. Usually the
simple act of opening up allows
the other person to feel safe in sharing.

3
Facing your fears shows you the bravery and strength
of which you are capable.

4
Push yourself through the first three minutes of the
fight or flight response.

5
Thank people for allowing you to be you.

Chapter 4

Hey, You're Naked!

Body-Image & How We See Ourselves Without Any
Clothes

Look around. There are things in your life weighing you
down.

Weight, and the dialogue around it in our society, is
one of my least favorite topics ever. I debated putting it in
this book at all since I feel even my acknowledging the
topic fans the flames. However, I know from my research
and from my readers, that weight and body image are often
huge factors in anxiety over dating.

With everything in life, we can always be too
something. As in, I could sit here and tell you I am too
short. Too bony. Too little-assed. Too shy. Too hard on
myself. Too scared. Too lazy in the morning. Too curious
as to why my breasts have started to look a little saggy now
that I'm nearing thirty and oh my god is this what my
future holds for me quick perk back up boobs!

But we need to pay close attention to how we see ourselves. We need to keep tabs on how we talk to ourselves.

Shedding the External Pounds

Look around you and start paying attention to what makes you feel bad.

That magazine that promises to give you the secret to a flatter stomach? Do you finish reading it and feel awesome? If not, throw it out. Don't pick up another one.

That friend who analyzes and picks apart every item of food you eat, who whines about not burning enough calories or how they wish they looked like a willow tree (I once heard someone say this, for reals) – how do you feel after spending time with this person? If you don't feel better, find some distance.

Often we have a distorted view of what makes us feel better. Maybe we have anxiety over the way we look and all the articles in magazines and models on TV help reinforce our insecurities, therefore leaving us feeling "right." Try to understand what it is you are seeking as far as validation or reinforcement. Sometimes, those emotions don't have our best interest at heart.

I've seen people whose partner makes negative comments about their physical appearance, then laughs it off as a joke. *Hey, you're too sensitive. Don't take everything I say so seriously.* This, to put it eloquently, is bullshit.

Repeat after me: I deserve to surround myself with people who make me feel healthier and happier.

One of the first big steps I took to pursuing a better relationship with my body was throwing out everything in my life that made me feel bad about my body. I started with my scale. I haven't owned a scale in over ten years. Now, I

38

only know how much I weigh if I visit a doctor's office and they make me stand on a scale. It's easy to become a slave to a number. It's easy to become a slave to the idea of a certain number. And it's easy to lose sight of the fact that our bodies fluctuate day-to-day, even hour-to-hour.

Use the focus you might direct towards a scale to creating a healthier lifestyle. What makes you feel filled with joy, light, and inspiration. Spend time listing off the reasons you are thankful for your body. What does it allow you to do? What has it gone through? What has it survived? Show endless gratitude towards your body. Train your thoughts to leap to places of positive thinking instead of negative.

This will take time, especially if your relationship with your body is an unhappy one. At first, it may feel forced. If your routine and habits include you putting yourself down or picking apart your supposed flaws, it may feel uncomfortable or even fake to start listing off all the reasons you love your body. But keep doing it. Every day. Maybe keep a journal that helps you keep track of everything you're able to do because of your body.

For example, I would sit down today and list off the following items:
1) I was able to be a warm cuddle partner for my cat this morning.
2) I was able to walk through my neighborhood to the store.
3) I was able to sit at my desk and work on a project I care about.

Like a filter on Instagram, change your filter for how you see your body. You want to choose a filter that focuses on what you are able to accomplish with your body, not on how it looks. If there are items in your life (TV shows, images, magazines) or people in your life (negative family, friends, or significant others) affecting how you feel about yourself, give yourself permission to seek some space. There are a lot of beautiful things for our minds to explore in this world. There is music to hear, art to view, books to read, conversations to be had, food to be enjoyed, and internet videos of cats to be watched . . . don't waste another minute disliking your body. Instead, use your body to seek beauty and adventure in the world around you. Go, now.

From Our Readers
I am a thirty-two-year-old man trying to figure out this whole online dating thing. I am bald (I started losing my hair at the end of high school) and am insecure about using photos that show my full head. I want to use photos of me in hats, but am scared of going on a date with a woman and seeing her face when she realizes I am bald.

Online dating creates conflicts of authenticity almost from the get-go. Before you've even started connecting with other people you are expected to define yourself in a description, list all your interests and beliefs, and figure out how much you want to share. I remember when I was online dating I really struggled with creating a profile that was true to who I was, but also felt like it would be appealing to the opposite sex. I remember slaving over striking the correct tone that balanced wit, intelligence, and a carefree demeanor (which, let's face it, I'm rarely "carefree").

We want to present ourselves honestly, but also have the ability to craft our profiles into our most-appealing selves.

My advice would be to present yourself in an honest light in which you feel most comfortable. While I also think any person who doesn't want to get to know you solely based on the amount of hair you have is a person you don't want to get to know in the first place, you should be engaged in online dating in a way that makes you feel safe. Use photos that focus on your smile, your warmth, and your openness. Use proper grammar and punctuation when you message someone. Show that you are a whole person beyond your appearance.

If you feel anxiety building up when you think about taking the step from online communication and in-person communication, I would encourage you to take that step sooner rather than later. It's tempting to postpone the face-to-face meeting as long as possible, especially if you feel you are clicking via email or text. But the sooner you move closer to authenticity by stripping away the safety of written communication the sooner you will learn if there is a possibility for true depth.

If you meet in person and you realize it might not be a good fit, graciously thank them for their time and honestly express you don't see it moving forward.

Trusting Someone Else With Your Body

"We barely even made out. Plus, you kept your sweat pants on the entire time."

This is an excerpt from an email I once received from a guy. We were in the middle of an email-breakup and I'd written something about being intimate and vulnerable with him. This prompted him to remind me that, whatever, my sweat pants were on the entire time. Years later I glance down and realize I'm *still* wearing sweat pants. Basically my biggest goal in life is to be wearing pajamas at all times and apparently that was even true while I was making out with someone in college.

Trusting someone with your body is a step only you can decide to take. Your gut will speak to you, so listen. If you feel like waiting, wait. If you feel uncomfortable or unsafe, listen.

It takes an incredible amount of vulnerability and courage to share your body with another person. It means you will be seen in a way very few people have looked at you. It means you will be touched in places you've never been touched, your tongue will go places it hasn't been before, and you'll find yourself moving your hands around someone's breasts, penis, scrotum, or vagina and wondering to yourself, "wait, am I doing this right?"

Determine how you want to feel when you're with someone and hold yourself to these standards. For example, if you want to be with someone who makes you feel safe, find someone who makes you feel safe. Your needs deserve to be met, so spend some time figuring out what your needs are.

Something I am still learning, when it comes to sharing my body with another person, is being vocal in both my insecurities and my needs. I find it difficult to voice what I am thinking in physical moments. I'd be naked as the day I was born, rubbing my body in weird rhythmic patterns against theirs, and not saying a damn word.

This may be connected to my not feeling worthy of being heard or it's because in every goddamn movie the physical scenes are smooth and seamless. People who know what they're doing in bed are beyond words, like they are being guided by some genius puppet-sex-master. They are silent except for moans or cries of ecstasy. And they know exactly what to do and when to do it. I always worried that talking would ruin the mood. I already felt neurotic enough in my own mind; I didn't want to spread it. There's no condom for crazy brain.

42

But it got to a point where I felt like I was faking it – not it, but everything. So I started to admit there were certain things I'd never tried before. For example, the first time I gave a man a blowjob I told him it was my first time giving a blow job. I mean, obviously I didn't tell him mid-act since that would prove a little difficult and I would end up sounding like that one chef-Muppet, but I eventually told him. I talked about it, why I'd waited so long, and why it scared me. And I started asking more questions during sexy moments. I began the process of trying to understand what felt good and why, so I could better communicate this to the person I was with.

By opening a dialogue about my body it created a more honest and real moment.

If you're unsure how to start a conversation like this, start by sharing some pieces of your physical history. What are some of your earliest memories of feeling desire? What were some sexy scenes in literature or film that pulled at you? I, for one, remember being crazy turned on by Steve Martin in that one movie from 1992, Housesitter. I don't remember the exact scene, but I'm pretty sure he was poking Goldie Hawn's boob, which in hindsight might not have been a sensual moment but instead a madcap comedic moment that went over my head entirely.

Either way, the more you practice openly discussing the body and physical intimacy and sex, the more it will feel natural and comfortable to you. It will also help your partner feel safe to share their thoughts. Who knows, maybe they too were turned on by Steve Martin's poking

Above all, when it comes to trusting your body with another person, you should never, never ever, ever, ever, feel like you need to do anything you're not ready to do. The person you are with will understand this if they are mature. If they are respectful and kind they will allow you the time you need. It is a huge red flag (are you listening?

43

huge red flag) if they try to make you feel bad about wanting to take things slow.

If they make fun of you, try to embarrass you, invalidate your feelings, or try to minimize the act, pay attention. That's dirty and manipulative and I would tell them that to their face if I could. Listen to your gut. Your intuition will be knocking on your door pretty loudly if something feels off.

It can be scary to stand up for yourself in situations like this, especially if you're trying to act like you know what you're doing. You may feel pressure from the person you're with, your friends, or yourself. But if you ever feel uncomfortable remember you have every right to stand up and walk away. Use a strong voice, find confidence deep in your lungs, and speak your truths.

Steps to Building a Better Relationship with Your Body

1

Pay attention to your self-talk and identify ways you want to change it.

2

Practice gratitude towards your body and everything it allows you to do.

3

Work on removing anything from your life that leaves you feeling bad or unhealthy.

4

Use your time & thoughts exploring things you love in the world.

Chapter 5

The First Time(s):

First Dates, First Kisses, and First Under-the-Underwear
Stuff

The first man I ever made out with, I only made out with twice. The first night we were with each other I kept my shit together. But by the second night, I broke down. We were in bed together and I started crying. Like, hard, ugly crying you see from people watching The Notebook and by "people" I mean me.

This was also the first man I'd ever kissed. And I really, really, liked him. Or so I thought. There were so many thoughts in my head, so many feelings coursing through my limbs, and so many unknowns. I felt overwhelmed. Since I couldn't find clear and mature words to express what I was thinking my body decided to communicate as effectively as it knew how. By crying.

Needless to say, my performance didn't get me a third date. And he ended things by email a few weeks later.

At the time, I blamed myself. I was furious at myself for not being better at controlling my emotions. I was embarrassed and ashamed. I was mad I wasn't more physically experienced. And my body communicated this blame and pain through even more crying for a respectable amount of time.*

(*approximately five full months of crying)

Years later, I'm able to see I didn't do anything wrong. We were both young and in over our heads. The moment provided a much needed reminder that neither of us was ready for a mature relationship. I don't blame myself. I don't blame the guy. It was just a bad recipe. Like trying to throw peanut butter into an omelet "just to see what it tastes like!"

Since then I've cried while in bed with other boyfriends and they've held me. I've had guys stick around the next day even after I've cried with them. And while I've moved past that first experience that was so deeply frustrating, that doesn't mean first times, the first time I do anything scary, doesn't still hold the possibility of some serious ugly crying.

Getting Your Ass to that First Date

As a child I used to dread going to summer camp. The entire week before I suffered from crippling stomach aches. Even though the camp was held at a local park, no further than a 10 minute drive from my home, it felt like I was being drop-kicked into a sandy pit near the Sahara desert, my mother shouting, see ya again never! I would feel a visceral dread any time I thought about the first day. It felt like I was walking to my death. I had no idea what to expect. I was scared of the camp counselors. I worried nobody would like me.

Fast forward to the last day of camp and I would be begging my mom to let me stay. I'd be devastated to say goodbye to my newly-formed friends and there you'd find me, sitting in the backseat of the car on the drive home, chanting camp songs like a brainwashed child of the Hitler Youth.

I think of this any time I feel myself dreading something new. I remind myself that the anticipation, the buildup, and the fear of the unknown will eventually be overshadowed by the experience itself. Even if something isn't as fun as a day at Disneyland, I survive and usually learn something. This isn't to say I don't still dread first-everythings like first days at a new job and first days at school. For example, when I taught English composition at a community college I always wondered if my students could tell that I was more nervous for the first day than they were. They must have caught on. One year a student wrote on my evaluation, "It feels like she tries way too hard to get us to like her." Story of my life.

But above everything else, first dates were always the worst.

If you're anything like me, the sheer emotional exhaustion leading up to a first date makes you question whether or not the date is even worth it. But it's important to remember that some situations we dread can turn out beautiful. We will never know if we don't try.

Try to find your own version of summer camp. Recall a time you took a chance on a situation that scared you. What happened? How did you feel afterwards?

It's always helpful to remind yourself you are capable of being brave. Whether you went to the first day of summer camp or finally saw a dentist after avoiding it for ten years, everyone has at least one memory where they faced a fear.

When it comes to a first date, I'd encourage you to establish the location of the first date early on. Then, go be present in that place on your own. If you're meeting at a coffee shop, go hang out in the coffee shop to familiarize yourself with the surroundings. If you're going on a walk in a park, go wander around the park by yourself and become comfortable with the environment. The better you can immerse yourself in the experience of the first date before it happens the better chance you have of getting yourself to that first date. It reduces the amount of unknowns you will face.

Next, practice a little self-focus. Start by establishing a reward system for yourself. Maybe you've wanted to spend an afternoon painting, but haven't found the time. Tell yourself that if you go on this one date you can dedicate an entire day to painting. Use this reward as motivation to get your ass out the door. A first date is as much about *you* as it is about the other person – never lose sight of this. Sometimes people can become fixated on what the other person thinks about them. We worry they won't like us, will notice the pimple on our chin, or they will be annoyed by how much we laugh. Stop. Reverse that. What do you think about them? You're as much a part of the moment as they are.

Finally, if you still can feel yourself wanting to back out of the first date I would encourage you to simply be honest. As I will many times throughout this book, I'm going to remind you that you can always communicate how you're feeling.

It's difficult to do. I know, because I often wanted to tell someone how I was feeling and then lost my nerve. I also know how scary it can be, especially if you barely know the person. You may worry what they will think. You may feel convinced that you will "scare them off" by admitting you feel nervous about the first date. But sometimes feeling pressure to act not-nervous on a first date is more exhausting than simply giving someone a heads up that you feel a little anxious. Odds are, they feel anxious too and will appreciate your candor. Being vulnerable takes courage. Be courageous today.

Being Mindful

It's easy to get lost in our own imagination. Our minds can quickly takeover a moment, dominate the conversation, and try to force us to function on autopilot mode. We may spend time worrying about the "what ifs" instead of being present in the moment and appreciating what is currently happening in our life. Have you noticed yourself doing this?

Being present in a moment, or the idea of mindfulness, is an active state of living. Instead of passively allowing your thoughts to control you, you instead make a conscious effort to engage with your life.

I spent the majority of my childhood in a constant state of fear over what could happen to me if someone chose to broke into my house and tried to kidnap me. I would lay in bed at night and wait to hear the fire alarm go off since I just knew our house was mere seconds away from burning down, taking every precious Lion King stuffed animal of mine with it. My thoughts were consumed by hypothetical concerns. What if I dropped a penny down the air vent and tried to retrieve it and got my hand stuck in the process? What if I swallowed my tongue? What if I pulled on my belly button in the bathtub and all my insides spilled out?

If I could have learned about mindfulness as a child, maybe I wouldn't have wasted hours wondering if the small noise outside my window was actually a mutant octupus trying to strangle me.

To start practicing mindfulness simply start noticing what is going on around you. It's goal is to anchor you in the present, to help you shift thoughts from hypotheticals to the concrete. Take note of the sounds. The smells. The temperature of the air around you.

By immersing yourself in the present moment you are helping redirect your thoughts to what *is* instead of what might be. You are derailing the autopilot attempts of your brain and taking hold of the steering wheel.

Research shows that if you are mindful you become "less evaluative" in your daily life and are able to connect with others in a more engaging way. Instead of spending that time worrying about what the other person is thinking about you, you are truly listening to their conversation.

From Our Readers
A guy I haven't talked to in person has just asked me out for coffee. We haven't even named a date yet and my anxiety is driving me nuts and it's all I'm thinking about. It's really making me want to cancel just to make it stop.

Before anything, start by reminding yourself that you are in control of your choices. You always have the freedom to cancel or decide against going. But also remind yourself that you have a responsibility to yourself towards growth. It's often easier, especially when it comes to our anxiety, to stay comfortable and avoid situations that heighten our anxiety.

This situation is full of the unknown. This is probably where the majority of the anxiety is coming from. If you've never spoken to this person, let alone spent time one on one having to talk and be a normal human being, it's almost entirely full of the unknowns. This is very, very scary. If you can, try and go to the coffee shop with a friend or by yourself just to become familiar with the environment. At least then the place will become known to you. Then, practice mindfulness – the act of engaging your thoughts with the present moment versus all the unknowns looming ahead.

For another concrete project start by writing a list of all the things that could go wrong. Everything from your car breaking down on the way there, to crying in front of him, to finding out he is your second cousin.

Then write a list of why you want to go, what you might get from the situation, what it might help you learn about yourself. Regardless of whether or not you'll end up clicking or going on a second date, what could you get from the afternoon?

There must be at least a small part of you that wants to do this, otherwise you wouldn't be contemplating it (or nervous about it). Once you can see these two lists side by side look at how small the letters are. Look at how easy it is to crumple up the paper.

It's also always a good idea to call to mind previous situations that you wanted to back out of, but didn't. Did you live through it? Maybe these scenarios were unbearably uncomfortable, but you survived. And now you have another opportunity to try something new. I only once went on a totally blind date. The days leading up to it were excruciating. I didn't go on a second date with the guy, we didn't click, but I also had a totally fine time with him at dinner. And I was VERY proud of myself after I got home.

Like I've said before, we anxious people need to encourage ourselves to adjust. Maybe don't trust your initial knee-jerk reaction of fear. Wait. Breathe. Try meditating and allowing your overwhelming thoughts to just float through

51

your mind like clouds. And next, encourage yourself
towards growth.

Thinking Outside the "Let's Grab Coffee" Box

Three loathsome words to someone with anxiety who is also trying to date: "Let's grab coffee."

What seems like a harmless and casual date to most people feels daunting to people with anxiety. Grabbing coffee means you have to sit. And talk. And figure out what to do with your hands. And where to look with your eyes.

How much eye contact is too much eye contact?

What if it's too loud and you can only hear 20% of the conversation so you spend the entire time fake-nodding and half-yeah'ing?

If you can't tell already, I am not a fan of the "casual coffee date." For someone with anxiety, there's nothing casual about asking the customer behind you in line if they could oh-so-kindly catch you if you happen to pass out. Yet this is the go-to for most first dates.

I understand; it's low cost, low stakes, and there's no pressure to stick around too long if it isn't going well. But good lord is it uncomfortable. I quickly learned that my anxiety didn't mix well with grabbing coffee. So I had to learn what I could do for a first date. This is something we should all understand for ourselves and adjust accordingly.

For me, my ideal first date is to go on a walk.

The main reason I love taking walks on first dates is that I don't have to sit still or stare at the other person. Keeping active allows me to fidget without my movements being noticeable. I don't have to obsess about making the appropriate amount of eye contact.

Even when a guy once asked me to get dinner with him I suggested we walk to the restaurant from my apartment. I needed those twenty minutes to decompress. The walk helped me calm some of my nerves.

Give yourself a break and say this out loud: "I don't have to grab coffee on a first date."

Make a list of places you feel comfortable. I have a friend who likes kayaking for first dates. Maybe you love bowling and the physical activity naturally generates conversation for the two of you. Maybe a movie sounds ideal since you only have to talk right before it and right after.

No matter what, give yourself permission to think outside the coffee-box. If your date is cool and wants to hang out with you, they should be game to try something new.

Anxiety After the First Date

You may notice that your anxiety increases after the first few dates. You may feel frustrated by this, or feel it is a sign that the relationship is flawed. But hang in there. Usually this is the adjustment period everyone needs when transitioning between being single and being in a relationship.

Whereas the first date is usually reserved for more surface level conversations, the following dates come with the expectation of reaching more depth. This is the point where we must start being vulnerable. Someone will start to really know us. And sometimes they want to touch us, like, in private areas. Real life (both emotional and physical) starts happening after the first handful of dates. This is very scary. And it's completely valid and understandable that your anxiety will go a bit bananas.

Questions will start bouncing around in your brain like: how to define the relationship? What do you want? What do they want? Where could this go? Where should this go? Will they still like me once they see me at my worst?

When you start being vulnerable, you open yourself up to being hurt. This is where the obsessive thoughts are coming from. The desire to protect yourself and your heart. I get this. I still experience this.

The beginning of a relationship can feel like it's out of your control. It's as if you're standing on a rocky mountainside: each pebble or rock beneath you is an intimate detail about yourself. You let one roll away to your partner standing at the bottom of the hill — no big deal. Another rock-detail rolls towards them, no problem. But then another gets away from you, then another and another. You start to feel the ground shift beneath you and you find yourself wanting to stop it, but suddenly the more that roll away the faster it starts happening and now there's an avalanche.

I think it's always important to remember that you can talk to the other person about how you're feeling. If the other person is understanding, they'll see this as a positive thing. I'm not saying you have to reveal everything right away, or share all your secrets, or show them the skeletons in your closet. But if you're feeling overwhelmed, just tell them. If you're feeling confused, tell them. If you're scared, it's okay to let them know. It's scary to speak your truths, especially to someone you are still getting to know, but you will feel better. It will also show the other person that you value them understanding your perspective.

Every man I've dated (or tried to date) I've told straight-up that I need to take things slow. I believe I once phrased it as "I need to go as slow as a 90-year-old grandma getting out of a low-riding car." And I always told them that I had anxiety. Some didn't handle it kindly, but most did. And the ones who handled me with kindness were the ones worth sticking around for.

Don't be afraid to simply say: I feel overwhelmed, can we talk about it? This may even make the other person feel safe to open up about their own misgivings or fears.

The First Kiss

In my freshmen year of high school we wrote letters to our senior-year selves. Three years later, upon opening my letter, I was surprised to find I had high hopes for my love life.

"By the end of high school I will have gone to a dance with a boy and I'll for sure have my first kiss by then."

I could hear my smugness screaming through the ink.

But by the end of my high school years, I'd yet to get my lips anywhere near another set of lips.

I told myself it would happen when I went off to community college.

It didn't.

I told myself I would have my first kiss at the very least before I turned 21 at college.

It didn't.

I didn't have my first kiss until I was 22. I remember feeling like I'd reached a point where I "should just get it over with." It felt like everyone in the world had already been kissed. But now I know, looking back on it, I was still so young.

Here's the thing — the older I get, the more people I meet who are late bloomers. I continue to meet people who have yet to be kissed, who haven't had their first kiss and are reaching their 30s. Or are reaching their 40s. And I find something beautiful about this. We are so convinced we must be the absolute last person yet to be kissed, while in fact we are far from alone.

Everyone has their personal reason for waiting. Some people choose to wait. Some desperately don't want to wait any longer. Some believe it will never happen for them.

Regardless of the reasons why, just remember there are more late bloomers out there than you think. It's easy to assume everyone around you is happy, or has everything figured out, or is confident.

The depression can feel real and raw when you start calculating all the people you know who have been kissed, have had sex, are married, have kids or whatever. But instead of comparing yourself, just take that time becoming the best version of you possible. The truth is you have no idea how happy anyone is. And the advent of social media has created a distorted perception of everyone's lives. We curate what we want people to see. It is visual manipulation. Remember this.

First kisses are rarely magical and perfect. And if you've waited a long time for your first kiss, the expectations may be out of control. You may feel like you've waited so long it needs to be really special or really romantic or with someone who really is Matt Damon (why you no return my phone calls, Matt??).

The movies make first kisses look gorgeous. Novels make them epic. But kissing can be gross. And hilariously awkward like when it's cold outside and your nose won't stop running or you sneeze right before going in for it. In fact, I almost started crying after my first kiss since it was so wet and weird. I worried it meant I'd done it wrong since I didn't particularly enjoy it. But come on. I'd waited so long to press my face against someone else's face that of course I ended up feeling disappointed.

Don't worry about being bad at kissing. And if your first kiss is less than spectacular, who cares. You can keep practicing.

Identify that you have probably built up the moment in your mind, and it feels heavier (and probably scarier) than it actually is. Show yourself grace.

Stop counting the years you haven't been kissed. Instead, start living and opening yourself up to life and possibilities.

First Time Sexy-Times

A lot of the anxiety I had when I was first entering the dating world, revolved around knowing I would eventually be expected to get physically intimate. I was terrified. The idea of being physical with someone left me feeling overwhelmed. I felt about as knowledgeable as a blind vegan trying to cook a steak medium rare.

Making out, hand-stuff, oral sex, and straight up sexual intercourse, all left me wanting to call up a nunnery and ask for an application. It all felt very scary.

Since I was entering heterosexual relationships, a lot of my anxiety centered around the penis. The penis baffles me. I tell Jared this all the time. Like, I'm really puzzled by it because it is so exposed, so vulnerable, and sometimes it moves without ANY control of the owner attached. It does things when they're sleeping. It does things when they're sitting in 6th grade math class. And I still don't quite understand how it decides which direction to nestle when someone puts on their undergarments.

For me, as a young woman entering the dating world of intimacy, the penis was like a grizzly bear sleeping in the corner of my living room. I knew it was there, I knew someday I'd have to deal with it, but for now I was mildly afraid and tried not to look directly at it.

A friend of mine in college once talked about how uncomfortable and scared she felt of her high school boyfriend's penis. At one point he got so exasperated by her discomfort he dropped his pants and said "it's just part of my body! It's just another body part, it's okay!" As a girl who hadn't even had her first kiss at that point, this story was both very amusing to me and very horrifying.

But it's also true.

It's just part of the body.

This holds true for all of us, and for all our body parts. It is just a body. Whether you are heterosexual, homosexual, bi-sexual, bi-curious, or anything in between, our body is just a body.

So much of my anxiety came from the fear that I would have no idea what to do at first. And you know what? I didn't. But that's okay. I'm being serious. Nobody knows exactly what to do at the beginning (or if they say they do they are lying).

My advice for anyone feeling this kind of anxiety: try not to stress it. Allow yourself to take as much time as you need. Find bravery in your voice and talk about your uncertainties with your partner. I know, I know this is easier said than done, but it's true. Be kind to yourself, kind to your partner, and try not to take things too seriously.

Above all, never forget, if you ever feel uncomfortable or unsafe, listen to your gut and either ask to slow things down or remove yourself from the situation. Which leads me to my next point . . .

Remembering Your Autonomy

Here's something I want you to remember. You are never stuck. You have options. Just because you walk into a coffee shop, that party, that movie, or that bedroom, doesn't mean you have to stay there.

Even if you are not prone to anxiety or panic attacks, you can still feel your anxiety intensify when you place yourself into new situations.

Often panic and anxiety attacks are triggered from simply the idea of having one — the fear of having an attack when you're out. These attacks can come along when we feel like we aren't in control of ourselves. They can be prompted by the unknown.

This can make us seek comfort and routine, it can cause us to fear taking new steps. Don't allow it to do this. Try your best to get outside in the world, take those first steps while taking a deep breath. But if you start panicking, leave. You are in control of your own actions. Who cares if the person you're with feels confused. If you find yourself worrying about making the other person upset, then your priorities need to be analyzed. Your first priority is you and your health. If the person you're on a date with is a compassionate person, they will still want to see you again.

I'm always pretty up front with people. I tend to just word-vomit that I have anxiety or I'm nervous. You are welcome to be honest with the person or people you are with. You can tell them you struggle with anxiety. OR you don't have to; make up an excuse. Tell them you aren't feeling well. You have to poop. You forgot to feed your cat. Whatever. Who gives a shit, really?

I once faked a phone call, pretended I got bad news, and drove away when I had anxiety building up on a date. It was fine. I hung out with the guy again down the road.

It's okay to spiral and to feel trapped. I mean, it really, really sucks, but allow yourself a few minutes of sheer horror. Then stand up, remove yourself, and be kind to yourself. Don't beat yourself up over it. Above all, you deserve kindness.

How To Help Yourself Through Your "Firsts"

1

Stand strong and tall in the knowledge that you can take things as slow as you need.

2

Practice being mindful and present in the moment.

3

There is no timeline.

4

Try your best to openly communicate your needs,
fears, and hopes.

5

Follow your gut and intuition like a blood hound on a
trail. Follow it.

Chapter 6

What Does It Mean to be Healthy?

Physical, Mental, and Emotional Health

Any time I can feel my anxiety escalating, I try to ask myself what is triggering it. I try to see if anything feels out of control.

"Slow down Hattie, does something in your life feel out of control?"

I ask myself this question often; I force myself to reflect on what is going on in my life, and almost always pinpoint something that feels out of my control.

I first was posed this question by a therapist whom I told about my emetophobia (the fear of vomiting). I struggled with the phobia pretty severely for about eight years of my adolescence. She almost nonchalantly mused, "I wonder what felt out of your control at that time in your life?"

It was like she'd thrown on a light bulb in a very dark room and there, in the corner, was a box labeled MYSTERY SOLVED.

My emetophobia escalated, and reached full power, right around the time my family picked up and moved across the state. Yet in the moment, and even after all these years, I never once saw a correlation between the disarray in my external life and my ever-increasing fixation on how my body felt at all times.

We often overcompensate for internal disorder by trying to control something externally. For example, some people might begin restricting their diet. Some people begin strict exercise regimes. Some people may obsessively clean their homes or fixate on physical ailments. Look around you – are there patterns in your behavior that may reflect a need to control your environment?

One of the most important steps we can take in caring for our physical, mental, and emotional health is to educate ourselves. Never stop educating yourself on why you are feeling the way you are feeling, what could be causing your emotions, and how you can achieve a healthier lifestyle. Now, I check in with myself any time I feel like the shadow of my anxiety is spreading wider.

Being Good to Yourself Even When It's Hard

I often feel frustrated with myself for being so sensitive. This usually happens when I insta-cry, without any control over my tear ducts — usually in a public place. Over the years, this reaction of embarrassment or frustration has been reinforced by people telling me I'm too sensitive or that I need to develop a thicker shell.

While yes, certain aspects of life may be a bit smoother for me if I was a tougher person, I also know there is value in my sensitivity. And the times when I feel a flatter affect in life, when I've felt "harder," are the times I also feel disconnected from myself. The softer emotions simply get replaced by other emotions, ones like anger or apathy. If you struggle with anxiety or with being a later bloomer, odds are someone has pointed out that there is something you can do about it and odds are that includes changing your personality somehow.

If there's one thing which the world needs more of, it's empathy. We need more people who feel, who connect, and who understand that life is complex.

If you're sensitive, it often feels as if your protective layer is less reinforced than others. Some people have these fortified stone walls, moats filled with snapping alligators, and men in towers who are awake and ready to pour hot tar on anyone who comes near. You, on the other hand, have alligators that are asleep, an exterior wall made out of sticks, and a weird troll under the bridge who tries to stop attacks with clever riddles. The emotions just come charging through, flooding your way of life and overwhelming you.

Before anything, before you can start working on your physical, mental, or emotional health, you need to remember to be good to yourself. Embrace the aspects of your personality that you may feel need to change. You need to lift all the parts of your personality you may want to hide or stamp out, and hold them up to the sun so they get nutrients and light. Often, what we most dislike about ourselves is the one thing the world is waiting to see flourish. Do you think Kermit would have gotten as far as he did by trying to be blue instead of green?

How Taking Care of Yourself Can Be Empowering

Taking care of yourself means you are acknowledging that you are worthy of caretaking and good health. I know some people cringe at the thought of "putting yourself first" since it feels trite. Or, even worse, you struggle with feelings of selfishness if you place your own needs above others. But it's absolutely essential to our well-being that we prioritize our own needs.

A lot of us feel pressure to express our love and devotion through action, by always putting the needs of others first. We fear being labeled as selfish or distant if we ask for time to ourselves. This dialogue is something I've explored a lot with fellow writers. Writing, a lot like mental health, demands a degree of solitary time. Being with yourself, devoting yourself to something you care about, and being unapologetic about it isn't something we always feel safe to pursue.

It's not unusual for people to feel embarrassed at the thought of asking for alone time. Whether you're asking to sit alone and write or you want to take a walk in order to process what is going on in your life — you may feel like it's not worth the trouble of even asking.

Here's the thing: there will always be something else you could do. Always. There will always be someone who, in one way or another, depends on you. Another task you could check off you to-do list. Another bathroom or cupboard waiting to be cleaned. Another screaming housecat demanding to be given a treat like a rabid piranha swatting you in the face with his tail (seriously, Scout, chill out). But here's the other thing: these items will still be there even if you step back and take some time for yourself. And you'll be better equipped to handle each item if you feel rejuvenated and healthy.

If you truly want to be the best supporter for the people and to-dos in your life, be sure and step away every once in a while to check in with yourself. Show yourself the same amount of love and support you show the people around you.

This, in turn, will remind you that you're important. And this will leave you feeling empowered.

The Negative Thought Party

One of the hallmark qualities of someone who struggles with anxiety is the incessant conga line of negative thoughts. And just like when you're in an actual conga line, you have a degree of awareness. You know what you're doing is sort of stupid.

People with anxiety get the pleasant experience of both having negative thought patterns and knowing the negative thoughts are irrational. So not only are you worrying about life, but then you worry about the mere fact that you're worrying. This makes dating an exhausting never-ending, conga line of picking apart everything you say, do, and think.

My daily routine often consists of the following thought processes over and over:

1) I will have an anxious-based thought.

2) I will identify that it's irrational or unnecessary.

3) I will feel upset with myself for having the thought in the first place.

4) I will tell myself not to be annoyed with myself, to go easy on myself.

5) I tell myself to shut up, that I need tough love otherwise I'll never learn.

6) I will return to the original anxious-based thought and rephrase it in a better light.

If you've heard about Cognitive Behavioral Therapy you know what I'm talking about. If not, let's take a quick refresher. Simply put, Cognitive Behavioral Therapy is a form of therapy that focuses on replacing your current thought habits with new, healthier thought habits. For example, if my current routine has me waking up in the morning and immediately listing off everything I'm dreading about the day, CBT hopes to train my brain to instead list items I'm looking forward to. It aims to change the script of my internal dialogue.

This trick comes in handy when you're trying to date. The pattern of your thoughts, primarily the constant over-analysis, is absolutely maddening when you're in the dating world. Even now, after being with Jared for years, I can identify how my negative thought patterns wiggle beneath the soil of our relationship. It's gross. The darkest times come when I'm tired, or socially drained, and I start to fixate on one little thing that bugs me. This one small item will suddenly give birth to another item, which then gives birth to another, and then another, and suddenly I'm covered in small itchy bugs of annoyance and resentment and I am fighting the urge to start throwing the bugs at Jared.

Do your best to keep your internal dialogues in check. Remind yourself that you have control over what the script says and know that you deserve to hear words that will help you grow.

Listen to Your Gut

In the middle of my 6th grade year my family moved to another city. I started attending a new school. And almost every day, for the rest of the school year, I had a stomach ache. I spent a lot of my time in the nurse's office.

Or going home. I can still distinctly remember one of my teachers stopping me during recess and saying, "If you're not actually throwing up you need to be in class."

This was nothing new. Even years before my family moved I can remember sitting in a doctor's office, trying to list off everything I ate on a daily basis, watching as the doctor took notes and nodded. I must have been seven or eight and as he peered at me over his glasses he said, "try cutting dairy out of your diet. You could be lactose intolerant."

Stomach aches have been my daily companion for as long as I can remember. When I was younger, before I understood anxiety and how closely it connects your mind and body, I was always convinced I was sick. This eventually developed into my full-blown phobia disorder.

I went years abstaining from all dairy. See that birthday party at the roller skating rink? See that girl sitting in the corner who is meticulously removing all cheese from her pizza? That's me.

One day, after realizing my stomach aches hadn't subsided since my dairy-strike, I started to eat cheese again. Almost two decades later I still count cheese and one of my favorite foods.

The moral of all this story is our stomach usually knows more than our brain. Our bodies are wise. Listen to it even though it's not always fun.

For the first full year I dated Jared I had to cut most alcohol out of my diet since it was giving me explosive diarrhea. I don't know the exact moment I decided to stop drinking beer, but it was probably around the time we were on a "romantic" weekend getaway in the San Juan Islands. We were driving in a remote part of an island and — like a lady — I told him I needed to find a secluded area to do my business. Actually, what I said was "if you don't pull over I'm going to shit my pants." But you get the gist.

As I hopped over a barbed-wire fence and scrambled into the wooded area, praying no farmers or cows were nearby, I heard Jared shout from the car that he loved me.

This, I thought as I pulled down my pants in broad daylight, was true love.

What anyone with anxiety knows is what a cruel and cyclical relationship anxiety has with our health. Our anxiety causes us to have health or bowel issues, which then triggers a new anxiety over the possibility of having another bowel issue. This, in turn, triggers a bowel issue. Over and over this will happen, around and around like the world's grossest Ferris wheel that you didn't even want to get on in the first place.

The only thing you can do is hone your listening skills. Get to know the clues your body is telling you. And learn to breathe.

When I can feel a sour bubble forming in my gut or stomach I close my eyes, take a few steadying breaths, and visualize a strong golden light flowing from the base of my skull to my intestinal track. The reason I do this, like I'm a hippie in The Valley of the Moon? I read somewhere that irritable bowel syndrome is caused by a disconnect between your mind and your digestive system. So I try to visualize these two areas connecting and being given light and strength. Does it help? Sometimes. Would Einstein be proud of my scientific theory? That's a hard "no."

Eating, Drinking, and Sleeping: We're all just bigger versions of babies

What foods make you feel healthy? What beverages make you feel strong? How much sleep are you allowing yourself every night?

These are questions you should be asking yourself on a regular basis, then responding with a direction that improves how you feel every day. There's a theory in psychology, developed by Maslow, that our needs exist in a hierarchy. And if we ever want to reach the highest level, self-actualization (the pursuit of things that make us feel fulfilled), it's important our other needs are met first. At the bottom of the pyramid, the needs we have to first meet before anything else can be pursued are basic human needs. This means things like food, water, shelter, health and safety, etc. If we aren't fulfilling these needs it's difficult to reach your dream of becoming a world class magician.

In order to help take care of your anxiety, you should first need to take care of your basic needs. Listen to what you need. Make adjustments as you go along.

Because it made me feel healthier, I basically cut all caffeine out of my diet a few years back. I also avoid lots of sugary things and don't eat a ton of meat. People always want to know my reasons for these choices ("yeah, but why don't you eat that?") but really? I just feel better. And it seems to make my brain feel healthier, too.

Diet is a personal choice that should be adjusted according to your own personal needs. This is why I'm not a huge fan of fad diets or anyone telling someone else "you should never eat X, Y, or Z." If you pay enough attention to your body, it will tell you what makes you feel healthier. Sometimes it takes a little time, particularly if your body is used to being given large amounts of something every day — especially when it comes to sugar and caffeine — but that doesn't mean it's not worth trying a change if it's what you want.

Another area to pay attention to is the amount of sleep you get. In today's world, there is always one-more-thing to do right before bed (and/or one more episode of House Hunters to watch) but the quality of our sleep directly impacts the quality of our cognitive functioning. Lack of sleep may, hypothetically, result in someone becoming irrationally angry when a person demands their new home have granite counter tops but then complains to the realtor that it's not the right color of granite (I'm just saying that could happen hypothetically).

When Jared and I first started dating I often went to sleep around 8:30pm, which was a stark contrast to Jared's average bedtime of midnight. He'd ask me to go see a movie and I'd joke "dinner at 4:30 and a movie at 5:30?" But really, it wasn't a joke. The anxiety of getting to know someone new, the disruption of my daily routine, and trying to consciously appreciate the present moment, left me exhausted by sunset.

Living with anxiety is tiring. If you can feel yourself fatiguing do your best to allow yourself a little extra rest. Be sure to give yourself plenty of time to recuperate from your day.

Be good to yourself. Drink lots of water. Reach for colorful vegetables and fruit that connect you to the earth. Slice up that avocado like it's your bitch then give yourself permission to go to bed early.

The Great Depression

If depression were Batman, then anxiety would be Robin. They usually can be found together fighting crime, except instead of fighting crime they are on the couch in sweatpants not showering and criticizing each other.

My first encounter with depression occurred in high school, though I didn't really know it at the time. It wasn't until we read Charlotte Perkin Gilman's story "The Yellow Wallpaper" in senior English that I went "huh, this feels familiar." Homegirl wasn't feeling great and neither was I.

Depression usually involves someone losing interest in the things that used to bring them joy. There may be a loss of appetite, a change in sleep patterns, and a change in weight. People with depression may become irritable or angry. There's usually a lot of fatigue that comes along with it. It may be difficult to make decisions or to take action.

Since high school, I've been able to better identify when I'm entering an age of depression. I like calling it an age because then I can say things like "much like the Ice Age, this age of depression leaves me feeling a bit cold too thank you I'm here all night" and then the audience cracks a faint smile and by audience I mean my own face in the mirror. Seriously, I'm standing here in front of this mirror all night.

Depression is difficult to explain to anyone who has not experienced it. The people in your life may struggle to find the right way to help. They may accidentally say things that are more hurtful than helpful. They may be confused. They may act annoyed.

I wish I could provide awesome advice for someone going through depression. I guess I could encourage you to speak with a therapist, to go out in nature more, to find a physical activity you enjoy, to cuddle more, to watch more stand-up comedy, drink more tea, do some damn yoga, eat more kale, bathe, sing, dance, etc etc etc, but honestly every person's experience with depression is personal. These are all things I've tried and have worked for me to various degrees. But to be frank, I'm still dealing with it in my life.

For me, my ages of depression come in waves. The tide will go out and I'll feel fine for a while. I'll scamper out into the tide pools, frolicking and collecting shells while admiring the colors of the world. Then, the tide will come back in and I'll be engulfed by freezing water. I'll shout through mouthfuls of sea water, "this again!?"

So instead of me trying to eloquently stumble through advice, let's have a little story time. Stop rolling your eyes. I see you contemplating scanning to the next chapter. Don't skip this part! It's my favorite part of the book. It's my favorite age of history:

In 1968 the manned mission of Apollo 8 left our planet to become the first mission to orbit the moon. The three astronauts, Frank Borman, Bill Anders, and Jim Lovell (be still my heart) were flying a machine that had less processing power than today's average smart phone. And they were going to fly around the damn moon.

Nobody had ever flown around the dark side of the moon. Nobody had ever seen the dark side of the moon. Basically, everyone was just crossing their fingers the astronauts could come around the other side and be able to make it home. But even the astronauts themselves weren't positive there would be a successful outcome. I'm pretty sure everyone gave the mission a fifty-fifty shot of success.

As they moved behind the moon, they lost contact with the earth. Radio silence. This was expected, but no less terrifying for the men aboard the space craft and for everyone waiting back at home on earth.

I think of this mission whenever I can feel myself entering an age of depression. I imagine the uncertainty, the fear, the unknown, but also the unrelenting faith that they could come out the other side. And they did (sorry, didn't mean to leave you hanging. Spoiler alert, they totally made it back home after breaking records as the most-watched televised event ever).

They passed through the shadow of the moon and came out the other side all due to the combination of faith and the sweat and blood of humans. This is how I think of my depression. I will enter into the shadow, drifting usually against my own accord, but I also remember that I am human and have a choice to work hard to get myself back out to the other side. Along with my hard work, I need faith. I need to trust that I will come out the other side. Belief is more powerful than we can ever know.

If you want to borrow this story, please do. Please imagine those men, tiny and floating within a sardine can, moving behind the dark side of the moon, and trusting they will make it back to the other side. Remember that humans are capable of pretty extraordinary things, even when facing something unknown or scary.

Ride the darkness. Come back home when you can.

How to Shape Your Life to Reflect Better Health

1
Remember that sensitivity means you have empathy, a quality the world needs more of.

2
You will be better equipped to help the people in your life if you first take care of yourself.

3
Alone time is vital. Don't apologize for needing it.

4
Rewrite the dialogue in your head to better support your growth.

5
Listen to your body and respond to its needs.

Chapter 7

Moments of Pain:

Breakups, Heartaches, and Unrequited Love

When my sister was planning her wedding, she asked me to read a poem at the ceremony. I decided I would weed through all my favorite love poems and find the perfect one to read. After all, I studied poetry in college. This is my jam. I remember plucking books off my shelf, thinking, "this is a piece of cake! I've got romantic poetry up the ying yang!"

Turns out? Love poems are depressing as shit. As least all the love poems I love.

Death. Illness. Infidelity. Unrequited love. Pain. Fears. How did I never notice this?

As I sat on my couch, I had to compose myself. I remember thinking it explained a lot. It was like someone held my face in their hands, looked me in the eyes and whispered, *this is why you have anxiety over love*. Because as literature and poetry has taught me over the years, love can fuck you up. It can bring just as much pain as it can joy.

But, my dear readers, breathe in deeply and still take steps forward. The only way you will ever truly know great happiness is to understand what true pain feels like.

Epic (Painful) Crushes

I have a history of absolutely epic crushes. These experiences were surprisingly full of a lot of pain. I'm talking crushes that lasted years. Crushes that tested the boundaries of reality, of logic, and of health. From childhood through graduate school I was a serial monogamous crusher. Like, hardcore.

Little did these guys know, but on my end we experienced a love so dramatic and rife with emotion that Shakespeare himself would have handed me his pen and said "girl, you need to teach me about love."

My high school crushes had absolutely no idea. Probably because I never spoke a single word to them. Wait, once I did say "that's pretty cool" to an art project one of them was working on (jokes on him I thought it was BEYOND cool) and another time I said "bye" to one as I left a room he was in. Smooth as shit.

In college, I interacted with my epic crushes, but in a weirdly intense way that I'm sure baffled them. I'd send uncomfortable emails, random texts that I sweated over to convey effortless wit, and suffered through a handful of hangouts-that-might-have-been-dates-but-who-knows.

As an adult, I can now identify the ways in which my anxiety helped me develop these insane, long-term, crushes.

Anxiety, and the chemicals in your brain, have a tendency to create repeated, obsessive thoughts. When those thoughts are not fixated on your usual anxieties, they

Sell your books at
sellbackyourBook.com!
Go to sellbackyourBook.com
and get an instant price
quote. We even pay the
shipping - see what your old
books are worth today!

00070940018

0007094 **0018** c-2
S-6

can latch onto an object of your affection. You can, in a sense, become obsessed with another person. It's as if you have stepped into a revolving door of thoughts and have a really difficult time stepping back out.

For me, these obsessive thoughts usually latched onto someone I felt I couldn't have, whether it was the silent and enigmatic artist in my graphic design class or the musician with the lazy eye who found me annoying. This was made most clear to me the first time someone broke up with me. I desired them more after our break-up than I ever did during the short-lived relationship.

My anxiety also held me back from ever taking risks. I couldn't even bring myself to look someone in the eye, let alone speak to them. This created a sense of comfort in liking someone from a distance, and feeding that attraction through fabricated scenarios in my mind. It's so much safer and mysterious to imagine what might be, instead of feeling disappointed by reality.

Anxiety often is triggered by even the thought of stepping out of your comfort zone. For someone who is new to dating, everything about the dating world is forcing you to step out of your comfort zone. It requires you to be vulnerable and open to being hurt. It can feel much easier to not even try talking to your crush in the first place and continue stoking the flames of your epic crush for months and months and months.

The thing is, sometimes loving from afar can be just as painful as being hurt by someone. You may end up feeling trapped or invisible or lost. Not feeling seen is a very lonely place to be.

Only when I started bribing myself, literally promising myself rewards for taking new steps, did I break my habit of long-term crushes.

Spend a few minutes and see if you have a history of epic crushes. They may not be as epic as mine were (JTT, I'm still waiting for you to call) but try and see if you can understand these crushes through a lens of anxiety. Then, be bold and try to take a few new baby steps.

Unrequited Love

One thing I learned amidst my epic crushes was the pain that can come from not having emotions reciprocated. Anyone who tells you that you need to be in a relationship to truly feel heartache or pain is a moron. You can love and feel loss from a distance. Just ask anyone who has fallen in love with a character in a book who then gets killed off. That shit stings.

There is the unrequited love you experience from afar and then there's the kind you feel up close. As you step closer and closer to the dating world you may develop friendships. You may spend time with someone with whom you feel a connection. They could be someone from a friend group, from a class, or someone who lives next door. Nonetheless, you find yourself looking forward to seeing them, you find excuses to bring them up in conversations, and you think of them while listening to certain songs on the radio. They are on your mind.

The only problem? This person doesn't have you on their mind. And you can tell.

I don't know how many times I went through this experience, but it was often enough that it became as familiar as the sound of a bathroom door locking behind me as I cried in yet another college bar.

It's understandable why people hold on to unrequited love for as long as they do. As we learned from my epic crushes, I was the queen of one-sided-love for years on end. There's a reason we fall for these people in the first place. Whether it's shared interests, similar senses of humor, or a physical attraction, there's always a valid and true reason you're initially attracted to them. And as Emily Dickinson reminds us, hope is the thing with feathers that perches in the soul. Hope is a powerful and truly beautiful emotion. It reminds us that we have faith in life. Regardless of the futility of an unrequited love, take pride in knowing that you are capable of great hope. Never lose this trait. It will take you far in life.

One of the best ways to help yourself move forward from an unrequited love is to take your blinders off. Often, we have a very narrow and focused vision when we are holding a flame for one person. We ignore anyone and everyone.

I get it. Nobody, at this moment in time, can compare to the object of your affection. This is fair. But what is not fair is for you to not be growing or exploring your other options in life. I advise you to travel alone. I encourage you to talk to interesting people. I support you in flirting shamelessly with strangers, buying yourself a new dress, and taking an art class. Maybe next time you're out, allow that shy, smiling guy at the bar to buy you a drink and actually answer when he asks you what you do for a living.

Unhealthy Moments

I sat cross-legged on the floor of the guest bedroom of my parent's home. I was 22, unemployed, and playing Mario Kart on N64. It was the year between college and graduate school, a year I spent wasting time, and the year I found Mathew. My cell phone lay on the floor next to me and I kept picking it up to make sure it was turned on. I'd texted Mathew hours before. And now I was waiting. As I waited I selected my next race, watched the countdown of lights while revving my engine, and tried to ignore the silence coming from my phone.

This was the time I had a half-relationship with a recovering addict. He was also living at home. He'd dropped out of college due to his habit and the only difference in our direction in life was he had a job and I didn't. Other than that, I think we both felt lost.

I remember the hours I'd spend waiting to hear back from Mathew. Sometimes days. We once went three months without talking. There was no clear reason. We didn't even acknowledge the lapse of time once we saw each other again. He'd just be gone. Radio silence. Part of me liked the uncertainty. There was an odd sense of comfort and control that comes with someone so unstable — does this make sense? I grew to expect disconnection. It felt certain.

The year I spent getting to know Mathew was the same year I truly got to know my own heart and how utterly prone it was to self-abuse. I craved being with someone who neglected me. I salivated at the silence and mystery. I chased after his apathy like a child with a butterfly net in a field.

I learned that waiting for someone to treat you right could go on forever.

And what scared me into eventually walking away was the fact that his treatment of me felt right. Since I felt stunted in my own romance knowledge and un-dateable because of my anxiety I didn't have high expectations for my love life. And because I worried I was unattractive since no man had made a big effort to be with me, being with someone who didn't treat me right felt right.

Do you know what I mean? There was a safety in being unwanted. A reinforcement of my deepest fears.

I would often text Mathew late at night. Sometimes he'd text back right away, sometimes it would take a few days, and sometimes it took months. Science says we grow more addicted to something that reinforces us regularly enough, but not every single time. Like gambling. If we hit a jackpot every time the anticipation would be lost. But knowing it could happen, and it might happen this time,

80

wait, try just once more, hang in there, it'll happen for you creates an addiction. It revs your engine.

I grew addicted to hope. I grew addicted to the possibility.

Pay close attention to what you are getting from a relationship. What is being reinforced from the relationship? Your fears? Your hopes? Pay attention to the person's actions.

I know better than anyone that the compassion and empathy we may have for someone else may cloud how clearly we see our own needs. I wanted to be someone who believed in him. I wanted to be the one person who stuck by him.

I became an expert at understanding — and therefore excusing — the way Mathew treated me.

And still, to this day, I don't hold any hard feeling towards him. I still think fondly of him and what I learned. However, I also know that I allowed myself to be neglected, undervalued, and used. It was important for me to spend time with him since it taught me what I didn't want.

I could have easily stuck around longer. Who knows, I could have dug myself in since I can be as stubborn as gum in your hair, and I could still be with him today. But I consciously put space between us. I consciously said goodbye and ignored his future calls or texts until they faded away.

It is not easy. Anyone who knows someone who has tried to break an addiction, or has tried themselves, knows it often takes multiple attempts. And for me, this was true. Even though I knew, objectively, that Mathew wasn't healthy for me, I still wanted to be around him. Mathew was like an addiction and I relapsed multiple times. Told myself I was done with him then found myself back next to him in bed.

It's okay. That will happen when you are trying to change something that is heavy in your heart. Don't allow setbacks to deter you from moving forward.

When I think back on my year with Mathew I remember time we spent together. But more than anything, I remember sitting on that carpet, the soft music of Mario Kart playing in the background, and my phone sitting silent and still beside me, representing everything I wanted to live for.

When Relationships End

I feel like I went through multiple breakups before I ever had my first, as-defined-by-the-book, breakup. You can experience breakups with friends or crushes or even family members. We learn what it feels like for a relationship to end well before our hearts are ever broken by a romantic partner.

However, that is not to say your feelings and experiences are any less valid when they happen. The first time it felt like my heart had been broken by a man I hoped to love, I cried for weeks. He was the first man I kissed. He had made me dizzy with his flirting and attention. It was during my last year of college and I remember barely being able to drag myself to class after he ended things. I lost a lot of weight. And I got to listen to friends tell me, "you guys weren't even dating," or "you barely even knew him."

Years later I'm able to look back and understand where my friends were coming from. Their statements were not inaccurate. However, they were invalidating.

If you are going through the death of a relationship, show yourself compassion and care. Allow yourself to feel everything deeply. People will come along offering words that are supposed to help, but instead hurt. It's like they gave you a gift basket and you threw back the wrapping, expecting to find cookies or puppies, but instead found a bunch of dead wasps.

I was 25 before I ever could officially call someone my boyfriend. It was the first time someone else called me their girlfriend. We took photos together. Like celebrities on the red carpet, we made our debut as a couple one evening in front of our friends, my heart racing and my palms sweaty. I remember feeling so excited to be able to show the world that this was my partner. He was smart, creative, vulnerable, and in just a little bit of pain from his past. All of this added up to me falling hard. The only problem was he hadn't fallen quite as hard as I did. A mere five months later I was helping him pack his car full of every possession he owned, so he could drive across the country back to Chicago. I wasn't going with him, literally or figuratively.

What's interesting is when I look back on this moment in my life the most anger I feel is at myself. I'm angry I helped him move. I walked up and down flights of stairs, carrying his life, sweating with each step, my heart breaking a little deeper, hoping my act of love would remind him what I would do for him. But really? It was a desperate act.

For almost a year and a half after I watched his car pull away I felt pain behind my rib cage. A YEAR AND A HALF. We were together five months. I missed him for over three times as long as we knew each other.

I wrote about him. I stalked him online. I wrote to him. I felt fresh heartbreak when I saw his new relationship.

All of these experiences were fed by my anxiety. My negative thought patterns, fears, and deep sadness all came from a place of anxiety. It rattled my core to feel so certain about someone, to feel as if we were moving through life side by side, only to realize we were walking in opposite directions.

But everything I experienced after he drove away was valid. Just as every heartbreak you will experience is valid.

83

It doesn't matter how long you are with someone, you are still capable of great emotion.

And if you are lucky, you will go through something like this. Not that I wish pain or unhappiness on you, but I wish you the opportunity to think you've known love. This, more than anything, will aid you in truly identifying and opening your arms to real love.

When your heart is broken and you have lost your appetite, when you cry so much you wrap your arms around your middle, allow it to happen. And then, tell yourself that you love yourself. Repeat it in your mind. Towards the end of my heartache for this man who moved to Chicago, I started telling myself, I love you, Hattie. I repeated it for days. Eventually, I started listening.

Above all, take steps forward that focus on you. I'm not saying you shouldn't give yourself as much time as you need to grieve and feel everything, but I am saying you have a responsibility to yourself to move forward even in the face of that pain. You owe it to yourself to continue to explore the world, learn new things, try new things, and remember that you are an individual who deserves to experience what the world has to offer. By continuing to do nothing you are giving the other person more power over your life than they are allowed to have at this point. Take back that power by lifting your chin, stepping into the sunlight, and doing whatever the hell you want.

From Our Readers

I am in my third year of college and recently came out of the closet to my family and friends. I've always struggled with social anxiety and hiding my sexuality has been a huge burden for me that has only added to my stress. I secretly was dating a man for almost five months and when I told him I wanted him to meet my family he ended the relationship. I'm heartbroken and

feel so anxious about ever putting myself out there again.

Before anything, take some time to realize how far you've come and how brave you have been. It not only takes great courage to live a life true to yourself, but to also reveal that self to the outside world. It's understandable that you're anxiety has been heightened over the course of all these large changes, but don't be too hard on yourself.

The anxiety is there because of how much growth you are going through – imagine the anxiety as a form of a growing pain. Yes, at this moment it is painful and difficult, but it means you are becoming someone stronger and bigger in identity. You've made huge, courageous, steps and you need to take a moment to celebrate them.

Instead of focusing on the what-ifs in regards to the future of your dating life, focus on surrounding yourself with the people in your life who love and support you. It's so easy to get lost in the anxiety that arises from trying to predict the future that we often forget to take stock of what is here in the present.

If you recently came out to your family and friends you are starting to write new chapters with all those relationships. These people are now able to know you fully and it's a beautiful time to create a deeper connection with them. If there are certain friends or family who are less-than-supportive of the news, move on to the people who are supportive. Move towards warmth.

Because you have been hurt you will probably feel anxiety when you contemplate being vulnerable with another person again. When this time comes, evaluate your concept of trust. While we usually associate trust as something another person provides for us (as in, I trust you) there is a different way you can look at trust. Turn that notion inward and learn that trust can mean you believe in yourself to survive what comes at you. While you may never be able to guarantee no person will ever hurt you again, you can trust yourself to have enough strength to survive that pain.

I encourage you to spend time fostering the "new" old relationships in your life as you process this painful breakup.

Steps to Overcoming Heartbreak

1
Remember, only you know how much time you need to heal.

2
Allow yourself to feel everything.

3
Keep a journal or video diary that helps you process and track your emotions.

4
Remind yourself, over and over, that you are worthy of a healthy and happy relationship.

5
Focus your time and energy on people and projects you care about.

Chapter 8

All Your Other Significant Others:

How Our Family, Friends, & Coworkers Can Affect Our Anxiety

It can feel damn near impossible to explain what it's like to live with anxiety to people who don't have it.

You: I can't control how nervous I am about this date.
Them: You'll do great! You have nothing to be nervous about.
You: I know, but I haven't slept in two days. I can't turn my brain off.
Them: Don't be nervous.
You: It's not that easy!
Them:…..
You: Sorry for screaming at you.

Nothing makes me more aware of this than when I talk with my mom. She just doesn't get nervous. I mean, she has serious stage fright, gets shy in big groups, and blushed horribly and easily as a child, but it's not the same. Oftentimes — with the best of intentions — her advice has just been "don't be nervous!"

I remember a breaking point in my anxiety. I was 20 and was applying to colleges; I started having major anxiety over how my vomit-phobia would affect my ability to live on my own. One night I started crying with my mom. I tried explaining it to her. I tried to explain how I thought I needed to go to therapy and how my fear of vomit and vomiting controlled my life and how I didn't think I could go to college.

Phobia disorders are very confining. They share similarities with OCD and panic-disorders. I didn't really know any of this at the time, I just knew I thought about vomiting (of doing it, seeing it, hearing it) every day. Basically all day.

My mother listened patiently, as she always does because she's a rock star at compassion, but it was clear it just didn't make sense to her. However, the next day she came home from work with a packet of paper. She'd looked up my fear online and printed off as much information as she could. She'd found an information understand what I was describing, she still made an effort to research it.

It was the first time I learned what I was going through had a name. And other people had it. Everything in the packet described me to the letter. It was like someone interviewed me and wrote down what I went through every day. It even explained what probably triggered the phobia (getting the stomach flu when I was eight when my parents were out of town, then getting it again while at school). And it was a turning point for me connecting with my mother. Even though she doesn't have anxiety like me, she cared enough about what I was experiencing to educate herself. It was one of my first, most important lessons in how to manage my anxiety: educate yourself.

Being Understood By the People in Your Life

It can be very isolating and possibly very hurtful to have the people you care the most about not understand what you're going through. Our friends and our family are supposed to be the people who stand by us. They are supposed to be the people who understand us. But they can also, sometimes inadvertently, be the ones to most often invalidate our anxiety. Them simply not understanding what you are describing can make you feel insecure or embarrassed.

First, you might need to stop hoping they will one day get it. Maintain the perspective that oftentimes it's difficult for the people who love us to hear we are struggling. Parents could dismiss your anxiety since truly understanding the depth of your pain could scare or hurt them. They may feel like they have failed you in some way or feel helpless since they don't know how to "fix" you. This may scare them and their comments to you may be their way of trying to minimize the scariness of the situation.

Most likely they don't mean to be dismissive of your experiences. And, even more likely, you are guilty of reacting the same way to someone at some point. For example, no matter how much Jared tries, he just can't get me to care about football. He was raised by Nebraskans and therefore is a red-blooded Cornhusker through and through. I, on the other hand, would rather listen to an old man passing gas than have the sounds of a football game playing in the background of my living room. (Also, I say this fully aware that it will launch a thousand ships full of

Nebraskans to my doorstep. But, knowing them, their instincts will kick in and I'll still be invited to a barbeque.)

What I'm trying to say is we all can't understand everything all the time. We are all guilty of being dismissive at one time or another.

To help craft healthier relationships, you might need to protect yourself by not sharing as much as you might want to. It's not always easy, especially if you want certain people to be involved in your life. But over time you will learn who reacts in a supportive manner to your anxiety and who doesn't. Give yourself permission to protect yourself, and your relationship, by being a bit more selective in what you share. Find people who make you feel lifted and supported. Find people who don't treat you like shit but instead are symbolic shit as in the fertilizer in your garden of anxiety, helping you grow and flourish and thrive and…okay, this metaphor is getting away from me.

Family Time

One of the first places you should look when you are trying to better understand your anxiety is your family. The relationships we witnessed during our formative years often help shape the way we approach our own relationships. The dialogue you grew up hearing, regarding love, intimacy, and sex often informs our own internal-script.

Take some time to analyze your family and the environment in which you grew up. What patterns can you identify? Were the people around you physically affectionate? Did they talk openly about their feelings? Did you feel safe to express emotion as a child? How was the topic of sex handled in your household? Do you have family members who exhibit traits of anxiety?

90

The better you are able to start identifying the patterns in your family life the better you will be able to start connecting those patterns to your own behaviors.

For example, if someone never witnessed their parents fighting they may develop a belief that conflict of any kind is bad. This may result in a submissive personality. The person may not choose to stand up for their beliefs. The person may believe that keeping the peace is more important than voicing their opinions.

Or if someone grew up being belittled or punished for showing signs of sensitivity, they may grow up to feel shame or embarrassment whenever they show emotion. This may make it difficult for that person to be vulnerable with an intimate partner. Or they may only be able to show sensitivity through aggression or anger.

We also have to navigate the dialogue coming from family. A lot of readers write to me voicing frustration over how their family discusses their love life. More often than not, people who are related to us feel a certain entitlement in providing commentary on our lives. They often point out that we are still single, as if we didn't notice. They may happen to mention how our cousin Betsy is working on her fourth child like some damn easy bake oven. Or they tell us we need to find someone nice and settle down.

I once had a friend whose mother regularly informed her that if she didn't lose weight nobody would ever want to marry her.

Another friend talked about his grandmother who offered to buy him a new car if he dated a girl for six months (he had recently come out of the closet to his family).

You hear it all — well-meaning family members who think their questions or suggestions are helping you grow.

It can become very tiresome to feel the people closest to you don't understand or approve of your choices in life. And while these people are typically coming from a place of love (cue the statement: "I just want you to be happy!") their behavior often makes us feel anything but loved. If you already have a small fire of insecurities inside over your love life, family often waddles over and throws an entire bedroom set of wicker furniture on that fire.

Be sure to stand firm in your choices. Clearly communicate that you are still someone who is growing and learning and who is choosing to live their life based off what feels right for you at this time.

Sometimes, there are people who will never alter their script no matter how many times you try to offer edits or rewrites. There will always be that third great aunt twice removed who corners you at family dinners and asks you why she can't set you up with the family accountant. No matter how many times you politely decline, she will badger you.

In these cases, the only things you can control are your own actions and reactions. Go into the situation mentally prepared for what is to come. Remind yourself that she has no actual power over how you feel about yourself. Go over the reasons you are still awesome. Find some inspirational quotes on being independent. Read them before you head into a family affair you predict may be draining. Look in the mirror and tell yourself you are doing the best you can and you are fine. Try to view her with compassion and remember she thinks she is being helpful. Then, when the third great aunt twice removed zeroes in on her target and makes her move towards you, start playing your favorite Taylor Swift song in your head and simply nod and smile.

<u>From Our Readers</u>
I'm spending Thanksgiving with my girlfriend's family for the first time...HELP!

This is very exciting; before anything, remind yourself that this is a great thing. It means your relationship is moving forward in a positive way. It means you will get a better glimpse into the world that helped shape your partner. But it also means your anxiety will probably be working in overdrive.

My first piece of advice would be for you to "fake it 'til you make it." This doesn't mean you should be phony. Don't become someone you're not. Just become the best version of yourself you know you're capable of being, even if it's difficult in the moment. Your girlfriend obviously cares about you and sees good in you, so make sure the family sees this too! So even if you want to curl up in a ball in the bathroom, or run screaming when you have to meet 5 uncles and 20 cousins, push yourself to smile. To shake hands. To say, "it's nice to meet you." You can do it.

If you start to feel anxious or fidgety, get yourself to work. Offer to assist with something. Playfully demand they let you help in some way. Maybe you can get silverware out or you can help clean dishes after the meal. Offer to pouring water for the guests. Ask if you could take the dog on a walk. Offer to help out.

If her family is proving difficult for you to be around, if they are crass or offensive or make you uncomfortable, don't be afraid to acknowledge this with your girlfriend. But do it in private and in a compassionate way. It's important you still show gratitude while expressing how you've been made to feel.

If you're only there for the day, try and communicate with your girlfriend about when you'll need to make an exit. Reinforce that it's important that you stick with that exit-time. Especially if you are prone to anxiety or panic attacks, having a firm deadline will give you something concrete to hold onto.

If you're staying the night, or maybe a few nights, make it absolutely essential that you get some alone time to recharge your battery. Whether it's taking a walk or going into the other room to "make a phone call" (aka just sitting and taking deep breaths for 20 minutes) whatever it is give yourself permission to take care of yourself. The holidays are difficult enough as it is. And the holidays are supposed to be all about grace and compassion, so be sure to show it to yourself, too.

And remember this above all else: deep down her family just wants to see their daughter happy.

Career Time

Once, for about seven months, I worked as a classroom assistant in a preschool. I'd always loved working with kids ever since being a nanny through high school and college. I worked for almost two years as a behavioral therapist for children with Autism, and I taught gymnastics for toddlers. But these seven months as a classroom assistant were the seven most stressful months of my professional career.

It was like sitting atop a dunk tank every morning and watching an eagle eyed three-year-old throw a ball directly at the bullseye, a knowing smirk on their face. Those little buggers never missed. Day in and day out. My day, from the moment I stepped into the school to the moment I walked back to my car, was exhausting.

I had just moved to Seattle, moving across the state to be with Jared, and was so anxiously-drained by my daily life I made zero effort to keep my health in check. I had no energy to do anything besides go to work and go to sleep. I wasn't taking care of my physical, emotional, or mental health. This was reflected back to me in my relationship with Jared, causing a period of habitual stress for us.

Oftentimes, our jobs dominate our lives. We can find ourselves spending more time with the people at our workplace than our actual family and friends. If you work a typical 9-5 job, you are with your coworkers 40 hours a week. Your work environment is a place where you hone a lot of the same relationship skills that will translate back to your intimate and romantic relationships. Work is a place you can learn about your communication skills, your handling of authority figures, and how to tactfully ask someone to clean out the microwave after they use it. It can also teach you what you want in life. It can teach you how you want to be treated. And if your work environment is unhealthy, it will most likely bleed over into your dating environment.

That's why it's so important to be aware of the ways your coworkers affect your health. Does a certain coworker cause your anxiety to increase? Are there people you trust and feel safe around at work? These are all things you should process and understand to better manage your health.

If there is a coworker who seems to cause you more stress than others, try to understand what about your interactions triggers the anxiety. Pay attention to how they communicate with you, how they treat your opinions or perspectives, and what their body language says to you. Learn to predict how they will make you feel, then develop safeguards against these interactions. For example, if a coworker always comes to you asking for favors regardless of your workload, practice telling them you would be happy to help once you complete the rest of your tasks. It might be hard to say no at first, but the more you push back the more your coworker will learn not to take advantage of you. We teach people how to treat us. This, in turn, will be a skill you can use in your dating life and beyond.

Next, try your best to understand where they are coming from. If a coworker feels competitive or aggressive, try and understand their perspective. Maybe they are insecure about their abilities and are hoping their loud actions hide this. Or it's possible they have financial or family stresses going on in their personal life and are trying to regain control through their actions at work. Or, maybe, they are simply competitive and don't know how to be graciously ambitious.

It's always helpful for me to look at the people who cause me anxiety through the lens of compassion. At least, I try to do this. It's not easy. Especially if a coworker doesn't show you similar consideration, it can be difficult to try and reciprocate. But the more you practice compassion and patience, the more this skill will become second nature. And patience and compassion is something all relationships need in the same way they need hugs or cheese.

Finding Kindred Spirits

I have a few sacred friends who also deal with anxiety. Their ability to "get it" during my more difficult phases has been invaluable to me. And all my closest friends, regardless of whether or not they struggle with anxiety, show me patience and kindness. This wasn't always the case. Over the years I have met people who run the spectrum of personalities.

It's not uncommon for people with anxiety to encounter individuals who are less than kind. It's especially common during years of adolescence, puberty, and young adulthood. During these years people seem to feel discomfort in regards to something they don't understand.

This discomfort might then translate into bullying, mockery, or invalidation.

Readers have told me about friends who make fun of them when they seek advice or help in regards to being a late bloomer. I've heard stories of friend's catfishing each other (pretending to be another person online, flirting with the friend, and tricking them into thinking they like them).

To put it simply: people can be cruel.

It's easy for someone to attack what they see as vulnerable or "weak," and often sensitivity or anxiety is viewed this way. While they are wrong in this perspective, they will still act on it. People are afraid of what they don't understand. Fear often translates into aggression, but keep in mind this does not equate strength or courage.

Do your best to block out their voices. The minute someone treats you cruelly, don't give them another opportunity. Either put distance between you and that person, or mentally work to emotionally detach from them. Remain resolute in your pursuit of not only better understanding yourself, but better understanding how you relate to the world around you. This puts you light-years ahead of the people who may choose to make fun of you.

View your social circle with respect and care, like it's a museum you own. You get to pick and choose what pieces of artwork are housed in that museum. Find the most beautiful friends, keep them close, share them, appreciate them, and only select friends who really hear the rhythm of your heart. You deserve to be surrounded by things that make you feel whole and supported. Your friends should remind you that you are worthy of love. They should remind you that the world is a breathtaking place full of possibilities.

Remember, you may not be able to choose your family, but you can choose your family of friends. If someone is making you feel bad about yourself you have the choice to put distance between you. It's not always easy, especially with how interconnected friends groups can be. I know throughout high school and college I would often try even harder to get someone to like me if they treated me in an unfriendly manner. This was backward of me, but I get it.

I've heard many people say they'd rather be part of the group and treated terribly, than be on the outside. This is understandable, but not the whole truth. Just because you step away from one group doesn't mean there isn't a better, healthier group waiting for you on the other side. It will probably take time to find and cultivate, but in the end it is absolutely worth it.

Over the years I've cultivated my friend group and value them above everything. When I'm spiraling and can feel my anxiety threatening to drag me under, I often sit down and write a long rambling email to one of my anxiety-prone friends. Just the act of writing everything down and sending those words to someone who understands is as magically healing as visiting any Hogwarts professor.

Be mindful of who you surround yourself with and remember that you deserve to feel supported and loved.

Steps to Surrounding Yourself with Supportive People

1
Some people may never be able to fully understand your anxiety, which is okay.

2
Safeguard yourself against anxiety-inducing coworkers by learning their patterns and possible motivations.

3

Remember that family members usually see their actions as helpful. Mentally prepare yourself for routine encounters.

4

Put distance between yourself and any friends who make you feel bad about yourself.

5

Find, nurture, and embrace friends who make you feel safe and supported.

Chapter 9

The Other Side

How to Be an Awesome Partner to Someone with Anxiety

I've had people ask how they can better support their partner who has anxiety. These moments have been some of the most beautiful moments for me, like watching a sunset while sitting in a beachy snow globe surrounded by singing unicorns who are feeding me crackers and cheese. Just beautiful.

The mere fact that people want to know how to be a better significant other is half the battle. Wanting to improve your relationship and better understand the other side puts you far ahead of a lot of other couples. People are busy. People get stressed. We tend to forget that being part of a couple means caring for someone else and being supportive and nurturing. There's the cliché that says we hurt the ones we love the most, which unfortunately exists as a saying because it's often true.

I find I continually need to remind myself that Jared is someone who deserves my care and attention. When you are with someone for an extended period of time, it's easy to start taking them for granted. Or to assume they know how much you care about them. Once, during a point of conflict, he pointed out that at times it feels like I don't hold myself to the same standards that I hold him. It hit close to home because it was true. I can be hard on him. I can lose sight of the fact that he is human and doing the best he can. I need to continually ask myself (and ask him) how I can be a better listener and be a better system of support.

Pay Attention

One of the best things you can do for your partner if they have anxiety (actually regardless if they have anxiety or not) is to simply listen. But really listen. Put down your cell phone, your iPad, your other tablet, and your laptop. Turn off the TV. Maybe set aside 30 minutes every day where there are no distractions, just you and your partner discussing what is going on in your life.

Talk about your day.

Ask questions. Ask how they are feeling about things. Ask if they are okay. Remain present and practice repeating back part of their statements to make sure you clearly hear what they are saying. Remember specific details.

When you're first starting to date someone with anxiety, it may feel a bit daunting to hear they have anxiety. You may not know what that means for the relationship. You may wonder how they will treat you. It may leave you feeling just as overwhelmed as they feel.

Before you get lost in a dark cave of uncertainty, simply ask the person about their anxiety. Remain open and curious. By showing that you are interested in better understanding them you are establishing that their anxiety does not scare you away. For all you know you may be the first person to have the strength to want to learn about their anxiety.

I once told a friend about a particularly challenging evening I'd had with Jared. I was emotionally drained and had received frustrating financial news from an insurance company. This news triggered a pretty lengthy vent-fest on my part, which spiraled into me worrying about my career and future and existential-who-am-I conversation (so, a typical Tuesday for Hattie). My friend chuckled a bit and then asked how Jared reacted. I told her he sat with me and put his arm around my shoulder and just let me talk. This answer surprised my friend. She was impressed that my spiraling didn't make him squirm or cause him to get upset. I hadn't quite realized it, but she was right. He is a badass.

This is what it means to be present.

To not shy away from something that might make you uncomfortable, but to simply sit and listen and show you still want to be around.

If from the beginning you make it clear you are someone who will show them patience and compassion, you will set the tone for the time ahead of you. You will be showing them you are unafraid of what they are going through. You are giving them a safe space, which is one of the most valuable things any partner can give another.

Adjustment Phases

Someone with anxiety is a bit like a wild animal.

What I mean is this: put them in a new environment and their instincts kick in, regardless whether those instincts are necessary or not. They might panic. Or start sweating. They may desperately want to find an exit route. They might even wish they weren't there. They may feel twitchy or even downright miserable. Imagine suddenly throwing a raccoon into the backseat of a car: he'll probably go apeshit.

Here's what I always tell myself in new situations: wait it out.

This is something you can do as well as the partner of someone with anxiety. Be patient and wait it out. Allow the person to adjust to the new situation. They will be experiencing new emotions and anxieties that may be unfamiliar to them. Give them some time to adapt.

One of the challenges of living with anxiety is it often acts like an overprotective hug; the anxiety holds you back and helps you put off even the smallest steps because it's terrifying and exhausting, yet the hug feels so familiar and comforting. It's easier to just stay in your world of certainty and routine. I know, even weeks and months into dating someone new, I've often longed for the days when I didn't have to think about anyone else. But I tell myself to wait. Just breathe. Wait.

As individuals, it's important to push ourselves to try new things. As one half of partnership you can also help encourage your partner to try new things. The only way you'll know if you can adjust to a new environment is if you test it out. If that raccoon in the back of the car had a bowl of food, some water, a nice blanket to sleep on, maybe he would eventually take a nap.

When you're taking new steps with an anxious partner, move forward, pause, allow them to communicate how they're feeling and maybe pause a little longer. Allow time for adaptation. Then, take another step. Then another. Gently nudge while respecting their needs.

The few first dates I ever went on were so stressful for me that I left them convinced the man and myself had no chemistry. I allowed my fear and anxiety to speak louder than my rational mind. But since I knew my anxiety would probably be going into overdrive from the first dates, I didn't act on my fears. I gave myself a few days.

Instead of texting the date the minute I got home saying "thanks, but no thanks" I just waited. And I realized it was my anxiety pushing me away from the situations, not so much the men. I convinced myself to try and go on second dates. The next few times were a little (not a lot) more relaxed and I had (slightly) better times. For someone with anxiety, that's all I could hope for.

Allow your partner to be the raccoon. They will probably freak out a little bit when faced with a new environment. But wait. Wait and maybe quietly hand them a glass of water and a blanket in which they can curl up and take a quick nap.

From Our Readers

I've been dating someone with a pretty severe anxiety disorder for a bit over 4 months now, and I would like to know what have been some of the best things significant others have said or done to help you with your anxiety, and maybe some things you wish would have been said or done to help. I'll be the first to admit it's really hard (but well, well worth it!)

It takes a degree of patience and resilience. From my own experience, the beginning of a relationship contains a lot of tug & pull on the part of the anxious person. The anxiety is such an uncontrollable, almost instinctual reaction that even if I genuinely like someone and am attracted to them, I resort to craving the past comforts of solitude and routine. Anything new can be interpreted as "scary" to someone with anxiety, so they often struggle with feelings of flightiness. For someone on the other end, this can be very confusing and frustrating. It can send unintentionally mixed signals.

105

When I read this question to my boyfriend he sort of squirmed and grinned. He said, "well now I'm wondering about all the things you wish I'd done!"

But we've been together for years and here's what he's done: he's been calm, patient, understanding, open to talking about my anxiety, unflappable when I cry, and endlessly endlessly optimistic about the two of us. He holds hope like a flame in a shadowy room.

The best intimate situations I've been in are the ones where the partner has been validating and patient. This means, if I communicate nerves or shyness, they simply nod and ask if there is anything they can do to help. On the other side, I've been in scenarios where someone has tried to minimize my emotions, made fun of them, or told me to stop making everything into "such a big deal."

Create a safe space for your partner to be able to talk about what they are feeling. Frame it as you wanting to better understand their experience, in hopes of being able to be part of it vs. outside it. Then wait — change is not always instantaneous and it's okay to breathe for a while to allow that growth.

And here's something I wish I could have told some of my would-be dates from my past: sometimes a person with anxiety just truly isn't ready for something in-depth. Late bloomers have a few more stepping stones in their pathway to an intimate relationship than other people, and some of those steps are taken alone. So much of it has to do with timing. So, as cliché as it sounds and helpless as it may feel, sometimes it truly isn't you. It's them.

*Be kind. Be resilient. Be patient while also being
perseverant — as in, if the relationship is something you
feel is worth fighting for, trust that instinct and wait
through the anxiety to see what comes out the other side.*

*But here's my most important piece of advice for "the other
side" — always stay centered in your own needs and your
own heart. Be vocal about what concerns you, or areas
you'd love to improve. If something is troubling you,
draining you, or confusing you, trust the strength of your
partner to be able to hear what you have to say. It's often a
misconception that people with anxiety are "weak" or
"overly sensitive" but it's wholly unfair for one person to be
walking on eggshells and the other to always run the show.
You deserve equal amounts of support and love. Remember
this.*

Emotions Happen

When I asked Jared if he had any advice for someone
dating a person with anxiety he paused for a moment. Then
he said, with complete sincerity, "sometimes crying
happens and there's nothing you can do about it."

While this made me laugh, it's also true. I cry a lot.
And usually there's nothing he can do about it. And yet
there is always something he does about it. He doesn't
shrink away. He doesn't try to minimize it. He remains
present and calm and unafraid. He allows it to happen.

This is huge, even if he doesn't see it this way. Strong
emotions can scare people, especially when it's occurring
in someone you care about. You may feel helpless while
it's happening. You may want to try and fix it, stop it, or
run away. Sometimes seeing someone cry may trigger
anger.

Anxiety can be an incredibly overwhelming experience. And it's not like other ailments, like a broken leg or bruised arm, where you can physically see the results. Anxiety is invisible and therefore a mystery to anyone except the person experiencing it. When anxiety overwhelms a person it often triggers heightened emotions. For me, this usually comes in the form of tears. Lots of them.

If your partner tends to show a lot of emotion, practice merely sitting with them. Do your best to resist any urge to "fix" the situation. Simply give them a safe place to express what they are feeling. Ask if there is anything you can do to help. However, if at any point the emotional responses become something that leaves you feeling in danger (for example, if the emotion is volatile anger that becomes physical) it's important to seek help. Clearly communicate that it's important for the health of relationship that they find safer, and healthier, coping skills for their emotions.

During times of heightened emotion or anxiety they may want time to process what is going on before they're ready to communicate clearly. Try asking them if they want to talk about things right now or if they'd prefer to wait until a later time.

Remembering Balance

One of the best ways to be a supportive partner is by always remembering your own health. It's important that you also feel cared for by your partner and that your needs are being met.

If your natural inclination is to nurture and help, you may find yourself focusing on always trying to be there for your significant other who has anxiety. Maybe you try your best to read their body language, looking for clues on how they are feeling. Or you make an effort to do something nice for them every day after work. And soon, you may find yourself choosing not to tell them about your own stressful day at work. You decide not to discuss your financial worries or the stress you feel over an ailing grandparent; you don't want to add to their anxiety.

However, this is not only unfair to you as an individual, but to the relationship as well. Neither person in an intimate relationship should feel their needs or concerns are less valid than the others. And yet, when living with someone with anxiety, it may begin to feel that your concerns pale in comparison to their challenges.

This is not true.

If your partner has anxiety and has ever made you feel your concerns or needs aren't as important as their concerns and needs, acknowledge how this makes you feel. Communicate that as one half of the partnership you deserve equal parts love and support. Never feel you need to censor your own emotions; if you communicate with kindness, empathy, and a focus on the health of your relationship, you are caring for the relationship. This is always a good thing.

Someone who has anxiety is capable of hearing what your heart needs and responding. Anxiety does not limit a person's ability to listen and care. Anxiety is not a "pass" for neglect or self-involvement.

If you both choose to be in an intimate relationship and both want to help improve your connection, then working towards an equality of support is essential. It may take time and diligence on both parts, but it well worth it in terms of strengthening the foundation of the relationship. Remember, always, to seek balance.

5 Tips for Being a More Supportive Partner to
Someone with Anxiety

1
Show strength by listening to your partner's fears or
anxieties.

2
Be present and patient during emotional upheaval – it
will pass.

3
Try your best not to try and "fix" the situation. Instead,
practice asking if you can do anything to help.

4
Remember you are also worthy of being heard and
understood. Be vocal in your own needs.

5
Remain perseverant if it's a relationship you believe in.

Chapter 10

Change Your Outlook to Change Your Dating Life

If you feel like your anxiety is interfering with your desire to start dating, you may also feel helpless. You may feel you've tried everything and there's nothing more you can do. I will remind you that you always have the power to keep trying. To educate yourself more. To adjust your way of thinking. Regardless of what you can reach for on the outside, remember that you have the power to change your thoughts and outlooks on the inside.

Being vulnerable with someone else and putting ourselves out into the dating world triggers our anxiety and fear. From this place of fear we may find ourselves pointing fingers out into the world, trying to identify the cause of the fear. By finding a name or a face for our fear we give ourselves the sense of control over it.

For example, during my online dating days I constantly reminded my non-single friends that all the guys online were creeptastic. When my friends told me to "simply meet someone online" I showed them examples of men whose idea of a conversation opener was versions of the phrase "hey u have a cute smile wana fuck?" I pointed my finger at all the less-than-ideal men messaging me (and ignored the few nicer ones).

Or, if someone had a difficult childhood, they may point a finger in that direction.

Or, if someone feels their small breast is what is keeping them single, they may point a finger at men-only-loving-big-boobed-women.

Or, if someone doesn't drink alcohol, they may point a finger at our culture's pressure to socially drink whilst flirting.

Or, maybe – just maybe – you point a finger at your anxiety as the reason you aren't finding romance.

Spend a few minutes and try to identify if you have recently felt a little hopeless as far as moving forward into the dating world. Take responsibility for your path and then own your personality.

The Best Place to Meet Someone

It often feels like this: If you're single, and want to meet someone, you're supposed to go to bars on the weekend and try to chat with attractive people like you're some James Bond of your local neighborhood. Be cool.

But what if you don't like going to bars? Or you've been going to bars for years and years and years and have never come close to meeting anyone? Or you prefer to stay in watching Netflix on your Friday nights?

You'll hear the usual advice. People might tell you to join a club. Join a gym. Go to a Farmer's Market. Meet through mutual friends. Speed dating. Online dating. Craigslist. Grocery Stores. Blind dates set up by your dentist (this is how I went on my one and only blind date).

You can force yourself to try every suggestion you've ever heard of where you could meet a potential date. You could drag yourself to an adult rock-climbing class where a

112

harness digs into your crotch as you attempt to conceal your shaking arm muscles. But the truth is, you will never meet anyone until you change the way you think.

The truth is there are endless places on this earth where you could potentially meet a special someone. Throughout history, people have met in every which way. People meet on dirty pee-filled subways, in grade school, in line for take-out . . . people meet. But it also feels impossible when you're on the other end. I know from experience.

When I joined an online dating website, I signed up for the most expensive one in hopes that the guilt I felt over paying so much would override my fear of going on dates. Yet, even though I was shown dozens of nice, friendly, appealing matches every day I found a reason to reject every single one based on their profile. One seemed too cocky. One had a ponytail. One used the wrong "there" vs. "their." I paid a lot of money to sit at my computer in my pajamas and blindly reject a bunch of hopeful men. Talk about a power trip.

It turns out, regardless of all the money I paid, I wasn't ready to meet anyone. But instead of facing my own anxieties and fears head-on, I found fault in every single match I was offered. It's a lot easier to shrug and say "well I tried! It's not my fault every guy I saw was fatally flawed and/or owned a scooter."

While, yes, you could probably meet someone online or at a farmer's market, those locations will look like an empty wasteland to you unless you have the right perspective.

The best place to meet someone new is from a place of open perspective.

It's okay if you're not ready to start dating (see the chapter on being a kickass late bloomer). But before you start huffing & puffing over how you're sick of the bar scene and it's so hard to meet someone these days, first do a little self-investigation. Try and gauge your level of openness. The height of your protective walls. The degree of your cynicism.

I'm not saying it isn't a clown car of misery trying to meet someone decent out in the world. It is. And you can't always control when or where you'll meet someone. But you do have control over your own perspective on the dating world. Try to stay open to possibilities. Sometimes putting on a pair of glasses that make you see the world through open-minded and bold eyes can make all the difference on who you see around you. I know for a fact I wouldn't be with Jared if I hadn't been practicing being open-minded when we met.

Finding "The One"

A few years back, while cleaning out my childhood bedroom, I found a list I'd written titled, "What my boyfriend will be like."

It was a list of characteristics. And it turns out most of those characteristics were physical. Oof. Embarrassing.

Apparently I wanted someone tall.

They had to be blonde or brunette. It was preferable they had straight, shaggy hair with some messy bangs.

He should have green or blue eyes. He had to own at least one suit. Maybe he could own a cabin. Be intelligent. Have a big family. Speak multiple languages. Was able to cook and ride a horse and on and on and ohmysweetjesus did I honestly write he should own several dogs preferably yellow labs?

If we're honest with ourselves, we all have "someone" in our minds when we think of our ideal mate. This is why eliminating people from online dating websites can feel so easy. If they don't match what we want for ourselves, we can claim we are sticking to our standards.

But here's the problem: holding ourselves to "the one" subconsciously, or consciously, makes us eliminate potential partners before we ever give them a chance. This is especially problematic when the reasons we are eliminating them are superficial. Not giving someone a chance because they have dramatically different political or religious views than you? Fair. But not giving someone a chance because they have curly hair? Maybe not so fair (just kidding, it's completely unfair).

It's easy to think that once we find someone who has X, Y, and Z, everything will fall into place. While it's important to have standards and to hold yourself to them, try and adjust those standards if you can.

The list could maybe say 1) respects me 2) makes me feel safe 3) makes me feel loved. Try to throw out your specific, descriptive list that states he should have Leonardo DiCaprio Titanic hair circa 1997. Try to take some chances. And, above all else, try to listen to your gut. How does someone make you feel? Sure, you always pictured yourself with someone who owns a sail boat, but does that computer programmer make you laugh? Listen to how your body feels after you spend time with someone. Do you feel better? About yourself? About life? These are the important questions to ask.

Throw your list out. Take a chance on that girl reading a book of poetry on the bus. Sure, maybe you've never understood a single poem in your life (although, seriously? Poetry is awesome) but that doesn't mean she won't make you happy.

Learning How You Define Love

What do you think Love should look like? What do you picture when you hear about two people falling in love?

Our culture conditions us to think about passion, fire, finding your soulmate, feeling as if you're losing your mind, maybe also losing your grip on reality. True love should be instantaneous and you should be fifteen, standing on your balcony, repeating his name into the stars above.

I remember the first time I heard about arranged marriages, I was appalled. I couldn't believe they existed. Yet research shows, in the long run, happiness levels and love levels don't dramatically differ between arranged and chance marriages. We know that intense, initial passion and lust eventually fades over the years. Yet we still crave it. It's like a drug.

Ask yourself how you define love. What you expect? What do you hope for? Some of our definitions might be distorted from our childhoods. From our relationships with our parents or friends. It might be distorted from the chemicals in our brains.

Write down what your first instant definition is — how do you define love. It can just be a list of words. Then, write down what you think love should be.

Chances are the first, instant, view of love might be a little immature or influenced by our cultural environment.

I imagine my lists would look something like this:

What love is: excitement, passion, desire, whirlwind, completion, spontaneous.

What love should be: steadfast, comforting, safe, reliable, honest, growing.

When I first started dating Jared I had to go through a period of adjustment. It felt different than my other attempts at romance. It felt quieter. Calmer. And, yes, at times it felt dull. I worried this meant something was off.

But this was only because my previous relationships had been unhealthy and unstable. The men I'd shared my time with before were all in a place where they didn't want a long-term commitment. But, because of the uncertainty that formed the foundation of our relationship, the experiences felt exciting. They were "exciting", but only in the sense that they left me feeling scared and undesired. They didn't want me and this made me want them all the more. I'd been guzzling desire-flavored air, thinking it was filling me up, not realizing I was still starving.

I had to do a lot of personal growth and analysis. What did it say about me that I felt more comfortable in a relationship where I didn't feel loved? Why was it easier to feel romance in instability?

Understand that love comes in different shapes and forms. Don't dismiss a situation just because you don't recognize the form it's taking. Remind yourself that you deserve stability and love. Your definition of love should reflect what you deserve from a relationship, not from what our culture tells us we should have.

Try to see your definition of love as fluid and evolving. Practice seeing it as something that can grow depending on what you learn and then change your definition.

Conclusion

Your story is a love story.

Living with anxiety is an experience that affects your heart every single day. I wasn't shown the X-Rays of my chest that afternoon when I visited the ER, but I imagine it would have been like every other chest X-Ray: a flat dark sheet that, when held up to the light, reveals murky outlines of bones and organs. The information and clues hidden within the film would have been invisible to me. I could have held my vital organs in my hands and not even recognized them.

While I wasn't able to learn anything new about what goes on under my ribcage from an X-Ray, I have been able to learn about my heart over the years. By educating myself about my anxiety and my health, by pushing myself to try new things, and by continually showing myself grace I have learned about myself. I've been writing my own pages to my own love story.

I hope the conclusion you come to after reading this book is the conclusion that you are capable of more than you think. That you are capable of greatness. That you are capable of finding love, whatever form that may take.

Over the years, I've concluded that as a person living with anxiety I need to live two lives. I need to live a life of comfort alongside a life of daring adventures. Because for me, sometimes just getting out of the house and meeting someone for a drink feels like an adventure.

You must take risks while also valuing what gives you comfort.

It's a lot to ask of yourself, to live with such dual energy. But while you encourage yourself to try new things you also need to show yourself patience and grace. And while you show yourself patience and grace you need to push yourself to try new things. Over and over this is what you need to be doing for yourself. Only you can make the choice to step forward towards romance. You owe it to yourself to strengthen emotional muscles that previously weren't given much attention. You deserve to experience life to its fullest and to grow and achieve new personal milestones.

I hope you walk away from this book believing in love and believing in yourself.

<u>Resources</u>

National Suicide Prevention Lifeline
Available 24/7 (1-800-273-8255)

The Trevor Project: Support and suicide intervention for
LGBTQ youths www.thetrevorproject.org

Project UROK: Mental Health support & videos from
College Humor writer Jenny Jaffe www.projecturok.org

Papyrus: Prevention of young suicide in the UK
www.papyrus-uk.org

<u>Books Hattie Recommends</u>

The Power of Now: A Guide to Spiritual Enlightenment
        By Eckhart Tolle

Joyful Wisdom: Embracing Change and Finding Freedom
        By Yongey Mingyur Rinpoche

The Power of Habit
        By Charles Duhigg

The Yellow Wallpaper
        By Charlotte Perkins Gilman

The Bell Jar
        By Sylvia Plath

The Harry Potter Series
        By J.K. Rowling

Calvin & Hobbes. All of them.
        By Bill Watterson

References

Alhola, Paula and Paivi Polo-Kantola. "Sleep Deprivation: Impact on Cognitive Performance." Neuropsychiatric Disease and Treatment. 3 no. 5 (October 2007): 553 – 567. http://www.ncbi.nlm.nih.gov/pmc/articles/PMC2656292/

American Psychiatric Association. 200. Diagnostic and Statistical Manual of Mental Disorders: DMS-IV-TR. Washington, DC: American Psychiatric Association.

Anxiety and Depression Association of America, ADAA. "Generalized Anxiety Disorder (GAD)." ADAA. Accessed May 28, 2015. http://www.adaa.org/understanding-anxiety/generalized-anxiety-disorder-gad

Anxiety and Depression Association of America, ADAA. "Depression." ADAA. Accessed May 28, 2015. http://www.adaa.org/understanding-anxiety/depression

Anxiety and Depression Association of America, ADAA. "Specific Phobias." ADAA. Accessed May 27, 2015. http://www.adaa.org/understanding-anxiety/specific-phobias

Beck Institute of Cognitive Behavioral Therapy. "What is Cognitive Behavior Therapy?" Beck Institute. Accessed June 5, 2015. http://www.beckinstitute.org/q-n-a/#q-n-a-70

Dickinson, Emily. "'Hope' is the thing with feathers – (314)." The Poetry Foundation. 1999. Accessed May 24, 2015. http://www.poetryfoundation.org/poem/171619

Harvard Business Review. "Mindfulness in the Age of Complexity." March 2014. Accessed June 20, 2015. https://hbr.org/2014/03/mindfulness-in-the-age-of-complexity

The Kenyon Review. "Jericho Brown Conversation." The Kenyon Review Conversations. July 2012. Accessed May 20, 2015. http://www.kenyonreview.org/conversation/jericho-brown/

McLeod, Saul. "Maslow's Hierarchy of Needs." Simply Psychology. Updated 2014. Accessed June 15, 2015. http://www.simplypsychology.org/maslow.html

McLeod, Saul. "Pavlov's Dog." Simple Psychology. Updated 2013. Accessed June 14, 2015. http://www.simplypsychology.org/pavlov.html

NASA. "Apollo 8." July 8, 2009. Accessed June 2, 2015. https://www.nasa.gov/mission_pages/apollo/missions/apollo8.html#.VYiWePlViko

Regan, Pamela. "Arranged vs. Love-Based Marriage in the U.S. – How Different Are They?" Psychology Today. August 1, 2015. Accessed June 10, 2015. https://www.psychologytoday.com/blog/the-science-love/201208/arranged-vs-love-based-marriages-in-the-us-how-different-are-they

Weinschenk, Susan. "Use Unpredictable Rewards To Keep Behavior Going." Psychology Today. November 13, 2013. Accessed June 20, 2015. https://www.psychologytoday.com/blog/brain-wise/201311/use-unpredictable-rewards-keep-behavior-going

About the Author

Hattie C. Cooper grew up in Northern California. She received her BA in English, minor in Psychology, and Master's in Creative Writing. Cooper founded *The Anxious Girl's Guide to Dating* blog in 2013. She currently lives in Seattle, WA where she works as a freelance content writer.

Find her online at
www.hattiecooper.com

Or on twitter
@CooperHattie

47645794R00080

Made in the USA
Middletown, DE
09 June 2019